brilliant
answers
to tough
interview questions

brilliant answers

to tough interview questions

Smart answers to whatever
they can throw at you

Susan Hodgson

An imprint of **Pearson Education**

London · New York · Toronto · Sydney · Tokyo
Singapore · Hong Kong · Cape Town · New Delhi
Madrid · Paris · Amsterdam · Munich · Milan · Stockholm

PEARSON EDUCATION LIMITED   Careers

Head Office:
Edinburgh Gate
Harlow CM20 2JE
Tel: +44 (0)1279 623623
Fax: +44 (0)1279 431059

London Office:
128 Long Acre
London WC2E 9AN
Tel: +44 (0)20 7447 2000
Fax: +44(0)20 7240 5771

Websites: www.business-minds.com
         www.yourmomentum.com

First published in Great Britain 2002
© Pearson Education Limited 2002

The right of Susan Hodgson to be identified as author of this work has been asserted by her in accordance with the Copyright, Designs and Patents Act 1988.

ISBN 0 273 65669 4

British Library Cataloguing in Publication Data
A catalogue record for this book is available from the British Library.

10 9 8 7 6 5 4 3 2 1

Designed by Claire Brodmann Book Designs, Lichfield, Staffs.
Typeset by Pantek Arts Ltd, Maidstone, Kent
Printed and bound by Bell & Bain Ltd, Glasgow

The publishers' policy is to use paper manufactured from sustainable forests.

Contents

WITHDRAWN

Acknowledgements

Andrew Chapman, John Dean, Robert Fox, Diane Goff, Geoff Hodgson, Les Hodgson, Margaret Holbrough, Andrew Perrins, Joan Sanders.

Introduction

Setting the scene

Going to the dentist, taking your driving test, sitting an examination, dealing with a double glazing salesman or attending a job interview are familiar experiences to most people. They also trigger predictable reactions for most of us — a sense of trepidation and a longing for them to be over and done with and for life to return to normal. In one case at least, that of being called to a selection interview, there is a great deal that you can do to alleviate this sense of anxiety and to turn the situation around to one that if not actually *looking forward* to, you at least feel thoroughly equal to dealing with. To begin with, you already have good news. You have been asked to the interview because your CV, your application form or your telephone call has struck the right note — you have whetted somebody's appetite and they believe you could be the person they are looking for.

The world of selection interviewers is not inhabited by evil sadists who spend their days planning ways of making candidates feel inadequate and stupid (at least, not in the majority of cases). It is peopled by hard-pressed managers, supervisors and human resource staff who desperately want to make the right decision for their organization. They do not want to cost their company time and money while a post is advertised again, a new short list drawn up and a training program started all over again because they inflicted a quiet and moody loner on their busy sales team or recruited a flamboyant socialite to work as a lighthouse keeper. Put

" Help them by being a well prepared, good interviewee and help yourself to give a really convincing performance. "

"Daunting and stressful as interviews may be, they also provide a golden opportunity for you to take centre stage"

like this, perhaps they can begin to win your sympathy and your understanding. Help them by being a well prepared, good interviewee and help yourself to give a really convincing performance. Even if, on some occasions, you don't get the job, you should come away feeling you have given a really good account of yourself and learn to do even better next time.

I am not saying that interviews are easy — they are not. They are demanding and stressful, and even if they sometimes seem low key, you are still being put on the spot and given this one opportunity to get something that you really want. Knowing what you are up against and what you can do about it is the essential psychological and tactical starting point for anyone who has been invited to a job interview. This is the case whether you are applying for your first job after leaving school, you have just completed a course at university, you are trying to make a change in your career direction, you are making a sideways move in your current employment, returning to work after time spent caring for a family or seeking promotion in your present profession. Regardless of what kind of work you are applying for, full time, part time, professional, practical, technical administrative, creative or caring you will have to convince a person or a panel of people that you are their ideal choice. To add to your difficulties, every other candidate will be trying to do exactly the same thing.

Daunting and stressful as interviews may be, they also provide a golden opportunity for you to take centre stage, impress your audience with your performance and gain the applause — or in this case, the job. Be careful not to take the references to *acting* too literally though. Showing the most confident and convincing side of yourself works well, but be careful not to create a false persona that is nothing like the real you. This puts a strain on you, the interviewer can almost always tell that you are not relaxed and natural and if you have to pretend to be someone you are not, you probably wouldn't enjoy the job anyway.

It is easy to neglect interview preparation as part of your general job hunting strategy. Preparing a really good CV and ensuring that you fill in application forms really well, combined with all your research on who to apply to and when to apply can mean that interview preparation ends up taking a back seat. Many people state that it is the paper part of the application process that they really hate and that if only they can get to an interview and talk to employers face to face they will be fine. As the invitation to an interview drops onto the doormat, breezy optimism flies out of the window. Talking to employers face to face isn't quite so easy. What questions will they ask and what answers will you be able to give?

This book will help *anyone* who has been invited to *any* kind of selection interview for *any* job to prepare more effectively, feel more confident and be well armed to deal with whatever questions, obvious, tricky or challenging, are thrown at them.

The chapters that follow will guide you through all the most commonly asked interview questions. You will find questions about you, your experience, your education, your interests, your ambitions and your personality, as well as questions about your choice of job and why you are applying to a particular company or organization. You will also find examples of unpleasant or illegal questions which some interviewers may try to use.

Questions without answers do nothing to relieve your anxiety, so each chapter offers examples of model answers which are likely to hit the right spot with employers. A model answer is fine, but it is just that, a model. It cannot realistically cover every single set of circumstances that occur in every individual's job search and career development. For many of the questions, you will find more than one suggested answer is given to illustrate how these answers have

"A model answer is fine, but it is just that, a model."

"Always think about what a questioner is really getting at when they ask you a question."

to be tailored to specific circumstances. Interview questions and answers are not mathematical formulae, there is never only one 'right' answer. This book also provides tips and exercises which will help you make the connection between the model answers set out and those answers which you would really feel happy to use and which describe your own circumstances.

Chapter 6, for example, on exploring your career choice, cannot outline every possible answer justifying choices of everything from accountant to zoo keeper, but it can enable you to focus on what questions you are likely to be asked concerning why you have chosen a particular job or profession and give you guidelines on developing suitable answers.

This book will be useful right across the employment spectrum. It is not designed only for those who are pursuing jobs in the commercial and business sector and will provide advice suitable for you whether you work in education, health care, commerce, industry, manufacturing or the media. In many chapters, you will find the use of the word 'company' referring to potential employers, but this is really shorthand for any employing organization with which you may be seeking employment.

The model answers are not intended to be learned as a script; if you try to use them in this way they will sound false, the answer won't apply to you 100 per cent and trying to memorize material will only generate a significant amount of additional pre-interview stress.

This flexible attitude which you need to employ in constructing your answers also applies to the way you consider the wording of questions. Always think about what a questioner is really getting at when they ask you a question. This book phrases questions in the way they are most likely to arise in job interviews and it also asks some very similar questions using different forms of wording to help you become more familiar with common interview language. Interviewers are human (even if there are some occasions when you have cause to doubt this) and they will have their own particular styles of questioning. "What are you good at?" "What are your strengths?" "What makes you stand out from the crowd?" These are all questions that are asking you to distinguish your major selling points — to demonstrate your assets.

When you attend interviews, don't be surprised if the language both you and your questioner use is less formal than that used in the examples in this book. Human nature is more idiosyncratic, more varied and more individual than any invented questioners and candidates. Naturally, there is a difference between a real conversation where you and the interviewer have hopefully begun to build up some rapport and a situation where specific questions and answers are being illustrated out of context. As a rule, interviewees tend to reflect the general tone and language adopted by their interviewer — this happens automatically, so candidates don't have to agonize and worry over whether they will get this right. In real, 'live' interviews it is often quite acceptable to include an element of humour, without trying to do a one person stand-up comedy show for half an hour. Humour is highly individual and candidates should follow their intuition and gut feelings about when to use it — it is not something that can be prepared for in advance.

When using the model questions and answers, you will find that it is often quite clear as to the kind of information the interviewer requires, so you won't find explanatory notes before or after every question and answer. Where, however, there is some doubt, or where additional pointers may be helpful, these are included, along with tips to help you focus on your own potential answers.

To ensure that you can adapt the answers to suit your own circumstances, many chapters contain brief questionnaires which help you

" As a rule, interviewees tend to reflect the general tone and language adopted by their interviewer "

"The key is drawing the positive out of the normal — the convincing out of the average and the extraordinary out of the ordinary."

focus on your past, your future, your strengths, your achievements, your values and your interests — all those things which matter to you and, when you are applying for jobs, matter to your future employer. These are not scored questionnaires that offer an external interpretation of you, instead they act as prompts and thought generators for you and will help your interview preparation.

You will find help in the following chapters to fit your particular circumstances, whether you have just left school or university, are seeking a change in career direction, returning to work after a break of some kind, or seeking an important promotion. The chapters are organized to highlight particular aspects of experience, education, employment history, interests, motivation and achievements, personality, ambitions and career choice and development.

Inevitably, because you are being given ideal models to work from in the answers, you may find the model 'applicants' seem irritatingly close to perfection since they are composites of useful experiences and personal qualities. Do not be daunted by these paragons of selection process perfection, sample questions and answers include examples of applicants who may not always have been successful and have not always trodden a straight path to career success. The key to all their answers and to all those which you develop for yourself is drawing the positive out of the normal — the convincing out of the average and the extraordinary out of the ordinary.

Your overall aim should be to become so familiar with any likely areas of questioning at an interview that you are unlikely to be caught unawares. You will be able to work out what the interviewer is really after even if the questions arise in different forms and most importantly of all, you will know what it is you have to offer and what you want to get across in order to maximize your chance of securing the position you desire.

All the questions and answers are based on what interview candidates state they find difficult and what employers say they are really looking for.

A final encouraging tip is that being interviewed is a skill at which people invariably improve and good preparation will undoubtedly accelerate this improvement.

look before you leap

what to do before the interview
and how to survive on the day

Never was the motto "be prepared" more appropriate than when you have been invited to an interview. Researching appropriate information, preparing yourself mentally and anticipating the questions you are likely to be asked are the key elements to success.

The greater part of this book is given over to anticipating the questions you could be asked and preparing concise, effective answers that will help you to stand out from the crowd. You will have to prepare for every eventuality, so you are unlikely to be asked everything for which you have prepared, but it does not have to be like a written examination where you have revised the wrong bits of the syllabus, it is possible to prepare for whatever is in your interviewer's armoury.

Remind yourself that almost all the questions you will be asked are designed to find out more about you, and, above everything else your suitability for a particular position and the likelihood of you

"Interviewers are seeking the answers to three fundamental questions: "Can you do the job?" "Will you do the job?" and "Will you fit in?""

fitting in well with the organization, its ethos, its staff and its work style. Whatever range of questions you encounter and in whatever form they are asked, all interviewers are seeking the answers to three absolutely fundamental questions.

Can you do the job? Do you have the appropriate mix of qualifications and/or experience to provide you with the basic skills and knowledge to do the job?

Will you do the job? A quite different question from "can you" — this question is all about your *willingness* to do the work. Are you keen and eager, how can you demonstrate your motivation?

Will you fit in? This is all about your suitability to work in that particular set up. Part of the answer to this question is hard to put into formal questions and answers; it is something you put over and the interviewer takes in at a more intuitive level. There are, however, whole sets of questions that do relate to this area — those questions about team work, dealing with difficult situations with other members of staff, being adaptable, flexible and friendly.

Tip

Don't waste your time working out which of these three themes your interviewer is exploring as he or she questions you, simply be aware that you want them to be thinking "yes, yes, yes" to these most fundamental questions as you prepare and deliver all your answers.

Given that the interviewer wants to know about you, make sure this is a topic with which you are comfortable and familiar. You may have come to take yourself for granted by now, so take time to really sit down and think about what your qualities and your strengths are, and also any weak spots you have that an interviewer may pick up on. Beware of doing yourself down. Many people are far quicker at listing their drawbacks than their plus points. It is essential that you do this as part of your interview preparation and the short questionnaire that follows will help you to focus clearly on your main selling points.

It is true that different jobs require different portfolios of skills and experience, but there is a hard core of skills and abilities that feature in many job adverts and on many job descriptions regardless of the position being sought. Your own common sense and knowledge of the particular field of employment concerned will help you work out what combination of these skills is most important for the kind of work for which you are applying. A psychotherapist probably needs greater listening skills than a chartered accountant, for example, and the creativity of an advertising copywriter is not the same as the creativity of a food technologist.

Work through the following questionnaire and rate which of the skills you possess. Be as honest as you can, but beware of being too hard on yourself.

Key:

0 = You do not possess the skill

1 = You possess the skill to a limited degree

2 = You possess the skill to a high level of competence

Selling point	Score
Good with numbers	
Good at writing business letters, reports, etc	
Good at creative writing	
Good at talking to people face to face	
Good at talking to people on the telephone	
Good at taking decisions	
Good at listening to other people's problems	
Good at advising and helping people	
Good at persuading people around to your point of view	
Good at solving intellectual problems	

Good at solving practical problems

Good at organizing your time and prioritizing your workload

Good at meeting deadlines

Good at designing on paper, with your hands or with the aid of computers

Good at building things to someone else's specifications

Good level of IT literacy — knowledge of software/hardware

Good at working flexibly within a team

Good at taking responsibility for your own actions and your own work

Able to work on your own without supervision

Able to follow instructions given by others

Able to delegate work to others

Good at explaining things to other people, teaching skills to others

Able to pay attention to detail

Able to work under pressure

Able to motivate other people

Able to use your own initiative

Able to think on your feet

Able to learn new tasks or assimilate new information quickly

Now look carefully at your list and where you rated yourself as possessing any selling point, then think of an occasion or situation when you have *demonstrated* this quality. It is irritating to interviewers when a candidate reels off a long list of what sound like very desirable characteristics, but when asked to give an example of where they have used or developed a certain ability, the candidate is left floundering — struggling to give an example and revealing the fact that they are good at reading adverts and job descriptions rather than that they are well qualified for the post. Be really rigorous about these concrete examples, but be flexible in the aspects of your life that you use to demonstrate these — work, school college, voluntary activities, interests, home and family are all a valuable resource for this exercise and it is less boring for the interviewer if your examples are drawn from a variety of situations.

For jobs where you have a detailed job description which sets out specific selection criteria or a person specification, ensure that you have relevant material to talk about against each criterion mentioned. Interviews based on these often require the interviewer to score candidates against each criterion, so don't miss any out.

You will find this book returns frequently to the issue of ensuring that you can demonstrate all your good points with examples. This is not only for the reason mentioned above but also because if you consider that if most interviews only last for 30 minutes maximum, they provide a brief snapshot of you. The greater the amount of evidence of your suitability you can draw from describing real situations in your past, the greater is the opportunity for the interviewer to make an informed decision. Research shows that despite the effort selectors and candidates put into interviews, they are

"Research shows that despite the effort selectors and candidates put into interviews, they are actually rather a fallible tool for measuring future performance — past performance provides a more accurate measure."

actually rather a fallible tool for measuring future performance —
past performance provides a more accurate measure. Unfortunately,
the fact that interviews are fallible does not mean you can take your
preparation any less seriously because they are still a major selection tool used by most employers.

Tip

If you know what you can offer and you can put it across effectively, you are
well on the way to giving a convincing interview performance.

In preparing your answers remind yourself never to answer with a
single "yes" or "no" Experienced interviewers will encourage you to
avoid this by asking open questions that oblige you to give a fuller
answer. "Do you like your current job?"' is a closed question
whereas "Tell me what you enjoy about your current job" is open.
Always behave as if you have been asked a question in this second
fashion, so that you don't slip into monosyllabic answers. There are
exceptions — if you are asked whether you would prefer tea or
coffee there is no need to offer a lengthy explanation on the relative
caffeine contents and possible medical benefits or drawbacks of
either beverage, a straightforward "coffee please" will suffice.

In anticipating potential questions and planning brilliant answers,
don't forget that some of your answers will automatically lead to a
follow-up question from the interviewer. Don't be disconcerted by
this, it usually means you have said something of interest and they
want to know more. If it is simply that they want something clarified, they will say so. The key to success is to rehearse what you
want to say, but not learn it off by heart. Recall all your relevant
experience, your unique selling points, your personal qualities and
strengths and any problem areas you might encounter. Become so
familiar with this material that if someone stopped you in the street
and asked you to tell them everything about yourself in the next 60
seconds, you could do so with ease.

Dress for success

Intellectual and psychological preparation for an interview is crucial, but there are other more basic, but essential aspects to consider. If you think that some of what follows sounds obvious — it is — but there are still countless candidates who let themselves down by turning up late for interviews, failing to read instructions about what they should bring with them and appearing in a suit that has not been to the dry cleaners for a year and still bears the evidence of at least three wedding receptions.

Good personal presentation is an absolute must. It also makes you feel much better, much more confident and much more in control.

Being dressed for success is essential. It is quite understandable that candidates worry greatly about what to wear, not wanting to appear too casual and yet being afraid that being too formal in appearance might suggest that they are stuffy and boring. It is still best to opt for the formal. If you turn up for the interview and find that staff around the office are fairly casually dressed, you can dress down when you have secured the post. Your formal dress will not count against you, whereas being too casual might give the impression that you couldn't really be bothered, that you are not taking the interview seriously.

Tip

American companies are especially hot on very formal dress, so if you are applying to one of these, be especially particular about your appearance.

For men, a suit is by far the safest option, combined with a smart shirt and tie and clean shoes. Women have greater freedom, so that either a suit or a smart combination of dress and jacket or skirt, blouse and jacket are all acceptable, but the emphasis is on smart and not too fussy. A particular issue for women is whether a trouser suit is okay and there is no doubt that it ought to be. There are still some companies who frown on this though, so try to get an idea beforehand from company publicity. Sometimes candidates let themselves down with scuffed, unpolished shoes or by carrying a lot of excess clutter in the form of carrier bags, magazines, etc; stick to a neat briefcase. All candidates need to consider the kind of organization they are applying to join. A city law firm may have a different dress code from a software design company or a food manufacturer but, as has already been stated, when in doubt, opt for formality. Company brochures or websites with photographs of the office or plant and the staff that work there can give some valuable pointers.

It hardly needs to be stated that excellent personal hygiene and good grooming are a must, but even these can catch unwary candidates out. One personnel director of a large engineering company commented on how many applicants for a whole range of jobs, many at quite senior levels, would appear very well turned out and presentable, with well polished shoes, smart suit, etc, but with surprisingly dirty finger nails.

Tip

If your hobby is gardening or car mechanics, let the interviewer discover this through a meaningful discussion, rather than through working it out from the clues you are displaying about your person.

If you are using fragrances, opt for small amounts and something very understated. No interviewer likes a cloud of scent to arrive in the interview room two minutes ahead of the candidate. Many people advise cutting out use of fragrance altogether, especially bearing in mind that these can trigger off allergic reactions in some interviewers. Avoid heavy make-up, excessive jewellery and boldly displayed body adornments (men and women). As always, common sense dictates what will be appropriate; a firm of management consultants will have different expectations to a youth support project or the cosmetic counter of a leading department store.

Ensure that your wardrobe is organized in plenty of time, that your suit has been dry cleaned, you have respectable shoes and that you are not using a supermarket carrier bag as a rather understated briefcase. Whatever the rules and niceties of dress codes, it is most important that you feel comfortable and at ease. However you dress, try to wear something that makes you feel stylish and confident, but you should still feel like you.

If the time is right

Plan your journey carefully, taking into account all the worst possibilities that public transport, traffic jams or limited parking facilities might conjure up to thwart your good intentions. Inevitably, there will be those occasions when even if you have done everything within your power to ensure arriving in plenty of time, something will happen to disrupt your journey. If this happens, telephone the company/organization *immediately*. There is a world of difference for them between sitting there wondering whether someone will appear or having the opportunity to reschedule the interviews and knowing that you took the most sensible action you could by contacting them.

You will find it disconcerting if you arrive too early, so have a cup of coffee, go for a walk and do some deep breathing to calm your pre-interview nerves. Once you have arrived at the offices where your interview is to take place, use the few spare minutes constructively, but not frantically. Make a little bit of an assessment of the place. Do the staff you meet seem friendly, relaxed, busy, disorganized? What kind of atmosphere pervades the whole place? Do they have literature about the organization, its products and services lying around for the browsing visitor? What information can you glean that you have not found out before?

Nerves are natural

It is a very unusual person who does not suffer from some pre-interview nerves and a limited amount of adrenaline in the system can enhance performance. Interviewers are used to dealing with nerves, but they don't all possess the skill to discern the difference between a slight attack of interview nerves and an overall nervous temperament. Above all, you want to avoid nerves reaching the stage where they interfere with your performance. How each of us deals with pre-interview tension is to some extent an individual matter, but deep breathing really does help and knowing that you have prepared thoroughly and carefully makes a real difference. It may be extremely useful to get a friend or trusted colleague (provided that they are not applying for the same position), to ask you some of the questions to which you have prepared answers, so that you can become more at ease with your subject matter

Say it without words

A good, well-constructed answer to any question loses its impact if that answer is given in a diffident, lacklustre sort of way that doesn't really match up to the content of what is being said. The non-verbal clues that you give during an interview say a great deal about you. This starts from the minute you enter the interview room (or even the building) — staff you meet there may be giving informal feedback to the interviewer or interview panel. Be pleasant to everyone you meet. Clichés are sometimes truths and a smile really does cost nothing, even if your stomach is churning and your palms feel sticky. It is always a good idea to rinse your hands just before your interview, so that you don't have a clammy handshake. If your file or briefcase is in your left hand, you are ready to shake hands without suddenly having to shuffle everything around. Make sure you use a good, firm, handshake without trying to convince the interviewer that you were the national arm wrestling champion for the past three years.

Nightmare to avoid

One candidate was greatly surprised when a lady dressed in a flowery skirt and cardigan who was offering tea to candidates actually turned out to be the chair of the interview panel later in the day. How glad the candidate was that she had accepted her tea graciously and had not made a pig of herself with the biscuits.

Seating arrangements in interview rooms vary — in part depending on whether you are being interviewed by one person or by a panel and also according to what your interviewer(s) prefer. Don't take a seat until you are invited to do so, then remember to thank your interviewer. You may find yourself in an easy chair with perhaps a coffee table between you and your interviewer, or you may find yourself on one side of a formal table facing your interview panel across an expanse of desk top and note pads. Don't be daunted — the questions will not be any more or less difficult because of the seating arrangements. When interviewers are taking extensive notes, a more formal set-up is easier for them. It is difficult if you are sitting in an easy chair, but best to sit forward — this makes you look interested and not too casual. Look at the interviewer when you answer your questions and if you are being interviewed by a panel look mainly at the person who has asked you the question — occasionally glancing in the direction of the others to ensure that they feel included in the conversation. If interview panels feel daunting, then bear in mind that you will only be asked the same range of questions as you would be by one person and that they are likely to have arranged in advance who will ask you what questions.

If you know that you have habits like twiddling your watch strap or ear-rings remind yourself to cut these out. Similarly, if you tend to make extravagant hand movements while talking, try to cut these back a little, but you don't need to sit on your hands in a desperate bid to eliminate all evidence of your usual communication style.

Listen carefully before you say anything at all

Most of the advice in this book asks you to think about the answers that you should give to interview questions and to anticipate, as best you can, all the likely questions in the various forms in which they arise. Before you can answer any questions at all you must make sure that you have really *listened* to what is being asked.

- Concentrate — don't let nerves stop you hearing what is being said.
- Listen carefully to what you are being asked — rather like reading an exam question before you put pen to paper.
- Don't interrupt your questioner.
- Show that you are listening actively, but ask appropriate questions to help the conversation along.
- Understand your interviewer's point of view — preferably without suggesting that they would benefit from counselling or therapy.

Nightmare to avoid

A candidate who was asked if she had any weaknesses, was not sure if she had heard correctly, but thought she had been asked if she had any witnesses. This resulted in a very confused conversation where it sounded to the interviewer as if she was summoning everyone she had ever known to state that of course she was of good character — the inference being of course that no, she did not have any weaknesses. It was only in a rare interview feedback discussion that this muddle was unpicked.

"Before you can answer any questions you must make sure that you have really listened to what is being asked."

Research suggests that the result of many interviews is decided by interviewers within the first two or three minutes in an interview and that these decisions are made at an intuitive level, being dependent on the rapport that builds up between selector and candidate. If this is true, then it means that those early aspects of non-verbal communication, smile, handshake, general demeanour are important. There is no mystery to this and the same rules of courtesy and common sense apply as with any other aspect of life. What is different, is that you probably think about it a great deal more than you would on other occasions. It is dangerous to become too paranoid about these aspects of your interview, to worry about whether you have just blown your chances because your handshake wasn't quite right or that you sat down in your chair a nano-second too soon. So long as you remain friendly, warm and enthusiastic you can't go far wrong.

Final tips for good preparation

1. Double check your interview date and time.

2. Read through your application form and/or CV, or the notes you made during a telephone call.

3. Ensure that you have read any instructions about your interview. Sometimes you are asked to bring something with you or arrive early for a tour of the department or production site.

4. Check your travel plans.

5. Make sure your interview wardrobe is in good order.

6. Complete any research you need to do about the job/organization.

7. Remind yourself of your key selling points.

8. Switch your mobile phone off — no interviewer wants to know which of your friends is on a train at the moment, or even that you are just about to clinch a highly successful sales deal; there is a time and a place for everything.

9. Be positive.

Chapter two

more than an educated guess

how to show employers what your education really taught you

Your education, to whatever level you have taken it, GCSEs, GNVQs, degrees, or professional qualifications, is always something in which employers are interested. Their degree of interest is dictated by how recent and how relevant your education is to the position for which you are applying. There are certain situations where it will form the basis for a significant portion of your interview. For example, if you have finished, or are about to complete a course at university or college, your potential employer will want to know something about your education — something more than the factual information you have provided on your CV or application form. Why did you choose the subject/course/university or college that you attended? What were you good at and what did you find more difficult? Above all, what did you gain from your studies that will be useful to your employer?

Here are examples of questions and some model answers to consider and adapt to your own situation. Many of these questions are equally relevant if you have just completed a professional training or practical/technical course of some kind.

Again, the interviewer's emphasis is likely to be on how you made your choice, how committed you are to it and whether it is something of specific use to their organization.

Q. How did you choose which university you attended?

A. I looked carefully at all those which offered the subject I was interested in. I took into account their teaching and examination methods and I also wanted to choose somewhere away from my parents' home where I could learn more about taking responsibility and being independent. I'd also heard some really good things about the facilities and the teaching from school friends who went there a year ahead of me.

A. I was offered my place through clearing and so my priority became to get a place on a course in psychology/engineering/business studies. It may not have been my first choice, but it has worked out extremely well for me, it was a good course and gave me a lot of practical knowledge. I could have studied another subject at a university that I would have preferred, but I am glad I stuck to my guns over studying psychology — it is relevant in so many jobs, especially this one.

It is then likely that your interviewer will follow up with a question such as:

Q. Tell me why you think your degree in psychology is relevant to this position.

A. For several reasons; the main one being that I opted for a unit on business psychology where we looked at many aspects of consumer psychology and I am sure that will be useful in your marketing department. Secondly, I had not taken maths beyond my GCSE, and statistics and research methods gave me a chance to develop my numerical skills and I find I am much better in this area than I had expected. Most of all, I think the course taught me to develop an inquiring attitude to many aspects of human behaviour, something that is applicable in every job.

For someone who has attended university later on in their career, an answer to this question might be:

A.   Attending university as a mature student I did have to consider somewhere local. For this reason I looked very carefully at the options on offer and I researched employment records and examination results pretty carefully before I made my choice. I arranged to talk to a course tutor informally before I submitted my formal application.

> **Tip**
>
> Your answers, like those three examples, should be positive. They fit different life circumstances, but they all show that the candidate took control of their situation, regardless of what limits or constraints they faced.

Q. Why did you choose to study architecture/accountancy/law?

(This question does not only apply to university courses, you can substitute any training course or qualification in a question like this.)

A.   I was very clear that I wanted to study something vocational with a well-defined career path at the end of the course and I was also keen to study something new — something that hadn't formed a large part of my school curriculum.

(In your own situation, you should be able to find something much more personal to say about the specific course you have chosen: what really triggered off an interest in that subject for you? This something may be related to school or college studies, an interest you have developed or a related piece of work experience you have had.)

Q. Why did you choose to study politics/English literature/combined studies?

(In other words, why did you choose something that does not prepare you for a specific career or point you in a specific vocational direction.)

A.   I wanted to keep my career options open, study something that I was confident I would enjoy and therefore do well in.

I was not ready at that stage to make a career decision, but I was sure that I would acquire a whole range of useful skills from my studies. I knew I wanted to continue my studies to degree level and I really have enjoyed my course and now I do have a clear sense of direction, which is why I have chosen to apply to you.

Q. **You are studying biotechnology, but you have applied for a job as a human resource trainee with us — why?**

(Do they suspect that opportunities in biotechnology are limited and you have just grabbed at another opportunity at random?)

A. I was good at science at school and I thought biotechnology would be an interesting new area to work in. I found though, especially through my various periods of work experience that I am far more interested in dealing with staff issues and solving business problems than I am in finding scientific solutions. It was a surprise to me, but other people have also commented on my business awareness and how I seem to have a good grasp of personnel issues. My manager in my last work placement mentioned this on my placement report.

Q. **Would you choose the same course if you had your time again?**

A. Yes I would. I enjoyed it, I gained a good degree and I am sure it has helped me develop a range of skills and personal qualities, I write more effectively, organize my time better and know how to seek out relevant information and that is all on top of the academic knowledge I have acquired.

A. Well, I might prefer to have done something with a greater emphasis on information technology, but I have really enjoyed my course and I have become very good at working to deadlines, working with others and organizing my own workload.

Q. Leaving aside your academic knowledge, what skills have you gained from being at university?

A. I have gained several new skills — organizing my workload for assignments, researching information, meeting deadlines and working on joint projects with other students have been some of the most significant.

A. Returning to university as a mature student, I have learned so much about time management and good planning. I have a young family and I have also taken on part-time work to help my finances, I have met all my deadlines and I expect to do well in my final exams.

A. Living away from home for the first time I quickly learned how hard it was to manage on a tight budget, but it has done me a lot of good and I have learned a great deal about taking decisions, solving problems for myself and I think I have gained a lot of common sense.

All three answers are different and highlight a variety of potential benefits. What they have in common is that they are all enthusiastic and all demonstrate that the candidate has thought about what they have gained from their experience. They also emphazise again the fact that many jobs and professions are seeking quite similar qualities and skills in their employees.

Q. We have employed graduates before and they have been fine with ideas, but a bit weak on just getting on with the job. How do I know you wouldn't be like this?

A. I had a part-time job in a local restaurant while I was studying and that certainly taught me a lot about dealing with customers, fitting in with other staff and spotting where there was work to be done. Working on a joint project with other students, I learned to take responsibility for my particular tasks and discovered how frustrating it is to work with people who don't do their bit. I believe I am offering you a lot of common sense work skills and my degree is only one part of all that.

A. I worked in a bank for two years before I went to university, so I was already familiar with a work routine before I started my course. The course has really added to my skills — especially planning my workload, meeting deadlines and working out answers to problems.

Q. Which parts of your teacher training course gave you most satisfaction?

A. The whole course was excellent, but my final teaching practice was really enjoyable. I liked the school where I was based, but my own confidence to deal with pupils and my ideas on how to teach effectively had really developed by this stage of the year, so I was able to put a lot in and get a great deal back.

Q. Which parts of your course gave you most satisfaction?

A. I was looking forward to the business studies modules on the course, but when it came to it I really enjoyed the practical applications of information technology to solve business problems. My project on developing a specialized database really crystallized this for me.

Nightmare to avoid

One applicant, who was on an environmental management course, decided to bring some lettuces he claimed to have grown as evidence of part of his practical project. His big mistake was to leave these pieces of living evidence of his hard work and success in their supermarket wrappings.

Q. Were there any parts of your course that you found difficult?

A. To begin with, I found statistics really hard, I had never enjoyed maths very much so it was a real struggle. I am really pleased I had to do this now because my numerical skills have improved greatly and I have learned a lot about how to tackle something I find difficult. I passed statistics with quite a respectable mark in the end.

A. At first being responsible for so much of my own time, it was very different from school and I was not used to it. I attended some study skills classes in my first year and acquired extremely helpful hints and tips on how to plan your work and your time. That sort of thing has become automatic to me now and I enjoy the sense that it is down to me to make something happen and produce the right information in time for a given deadline.

Tip

You don't have to imply that you have always been perfect at everything, but if there are subjects or assignments with which you struggled, only mention these where you can demonstrate an improvement or a beneficial learning outcome.

Q. **What made you decide that university was the right choice for you?**

A. I did think about whether I should work for a year or two first, but I was still enjoying my education, I knew the course I wanted to do and I felt that so long as I did some part-time work to help my finances and give me experience of doing a job, it would be a good decision. I like the idea of being able to get on to the career ladder quickly and really get going.

A. I had been impatient to get out of school and start earning money and making a career. I did not mind my job in office admin, but I noticed that new staff who came in with degrees and other qualifications would often start with a more interesting job than mine and I began to think a degree would be useful. Having had a break from studying, I felt a lot more motivated to go back and really get something out of it.

A. It was a big decision for me, at the age of 36, but I had always wanted to study law and I had always put earning a living, bringing up my family or other things before my education. It was quite a shock at first, writing essays, giving seminar presentations and sitting exams, but I have enjoyed it, done well and I know my experience of life and of other jobs has developed a lot of common sense and a real ability to work with other people.

Q. I see you have gone on to do a master's degree immediately after your first degree — wouldn't some work experience have been more useful?

A. I did weigh up both options, but in the end I decided to complete the academic part of my education and have that extra qualification to offer to employers. I like the idea that I can now concentrate on my job 100 per cent. I have done several part time jobs in a whole variety of places and these have certainly given me a good grounding in the basics of work. Also, my particular masters course put a strong emphasis on solving practical business problems.

Spend some time working out answers based on some of the ideas outlined above, but which apply directly to your own situation. Remember not to sound defensive in explaining your actions and choices. The interviewer is trying to find out how you set about taking decisions, analyzing information and assessing your own performance.

Q. What was the most difficult assignment you had to tackle while at university?

A. The most challenging was a 15,000-word dissertation and information sources I was using were very varied — the university library, Government departments and local businesses. I had to be quite persuasive to get some of the information I needed because I had my deadline to work to and yet I did not want to get on the wrong side of people who were doing me a favour. It was a really useful experience and I am far more confident about planning major projects now.

Q. How would you describe the contribution you made to discussions during seminars and tutorials?

A. Well the contribution I made changed and developed during the three years I was there. I was never the person who said the most, but I tried to make sure that what I said was relevant and interesting and I got much better at listening to what other people said as well, rather than just waiting to say my bit. I enjoy exchanging ideas and I can be very successful at persuading someone round to my point of view if I really believe it is worthwhile.

(Add an example of an occasion where you have swayed the opinion of a person or a group.)

Q. You have said a lot about your course and what you gained from it. What else did you learn from your time at university?

A. I was elected as a course representative on our faculty board during my second year. This meant taking responsibility for raising matters of concern to students with senior faculty staff, discussing those issues and where there was a problem, working with academic staff to produce a solution satisfactory to everyone. One major success I had was in helping to get the library opening hours extended, so that students with family or work commitments could benefit from a more flexible service.

Q. What were you like at preparing to sit examinations?

A. By the time I did my final exams I had developed a very clear working method with revision timetables where I would work on preparing briefer and briefer notes on the subjects I was revising and read through these so that they would act as very quick reminders for all the material I was committing to memory. I actually think that some of my assignments were a better preparation for work, because there was still a deadline to be met, information to be researched and presented, more of a test of my time management and planning skills than the unseen exams.

Q. You seem to have left your job search until after completing your degree — was this a deliberate choice?

A. Yes it was and I know it may seem a slightly risky decision. I really wanted to concentrate on getting the best possible results in my exams. It seems to me that how well you do is very clearly reflected in possible openings in the job market and I did not want to limit my opportunities. It has meant that I have been able to concentrate really hard on the jobs and companies that really interest me, doing plenty of research and even talking to people in the company wherever this is possible. Of course, I was also doing my part-time job and as I had a promotion there during the past six months this has also strengthened my CV and increased my experience.

Q. How did you finance your law course/town planning diploma/ marketing certificate?

A. I had managed to save some money by working for a year immediately after I finished my degree, but I did have to take out a bank loan as well. It would have been great not to have to go into debt, but I got the qualification I wanted and the course was really enjoyable and very practical and relevant, so it was worth borrowing the money.

Q. Why did you choose to study on a part-time rather than full-time course?

A. It was quite a difficult choice, because part of me wanted to get on and complete my studies, but I really felt that I would be better off both financially and in career development terms by continuing to work throughout my course and I have worked for the same company for the last two and a half years now. I know I missed out on some aspects of student life, but I compensated for this by making sure I never missed lectures, attending faculty social events whenever I could and developing friendships with students taking the full-time as well as the part-time route on the course.

The questions above give you some idea of the range of subjects likely to be covered. You will also find many of the questions related to your employment history, your personality, motivation and ambitions will draw on qualities and experience developed through your education — these topics are covered in chapters 5 and 6.

Make sure you have answers to all the following questions, however they are phrased by your interviewer.

Why did I choose a particular university/college/training establishment?

How did I deal with any obstacles that affected my choice?

Why did I choose my academic subject/training course?

How does my career choice link to my studies/training?

If it does not, what explanation do I offer for this?

What personal qualities has university/college helped me develop?

What skills has university/college helped me develop?

What did I enjoy most about my course?

What was I particularly good at?

Was there anything I found difficult about my course?

How did I tackle this difficulty?

Why did I choose to study, rather than go into employment?

In what ways has my course prepared me for employment?

Write down answers to all these questions, so that you become familiar with all the answers and can recall this information without it sounding stilted or rehearsed.

After school

If you have just left school with GCSEs, A levels or GNVQs, the questions you face may not be quite so searching, but employers will still be keen to know more about what you studied, what you were good at what you found difficult or easy and why you took the decisions you did.

Q. Why did you leave school as soon as you had finished your GCSEs; why didn't you stay on at school?

A. I did consider staying on, especially as my GCSE results were quite good, but I had really enjoyed my work experience at one of your hairdressing salons, so I decided I would do well to start on work I enjoyed as soon as possible. I like the idea of learning through work and I know this is a job I want to do.

Q. What made you choose a GNVQ in catering rather than opting for traditional A levels?

A. I was keen to stay on at school, but I much preferred the idea of doing something that trained me for a particular career rather than something open ended like A levels. I had a Saturday job in a café and I enjoyed dealing with customers and with food, but I thought this GNVQ would help me to qualify as a really good chef in the longer term.

Q. Which subjects did you like best

A. English, history and computer studies. Computer studies is the one I think will be most useful at work, I have had my own PC for five years now and I shall enjoy any job where I get a chance to use computers and develop my skills more. I would be quite happy to go to evening classes or do short courses to get better qualified.

Q. Which subjects were you good at?

A. I got my best results in science and maths. We had really good teachers for those subjects, but I don't think they are the subjects I am most interested in using at work, although I know the maths will always be useful. I did fairly well in most subjects though, rather than having one that was much better than the rest.

Q. Were there any subjects you weren't any good at?

A. Languages — I took French and German, but I found them quite tricky. I wanted to do well in maths, English and science and that has paid off well as I have passed all three with good grades.

Q. What would your teachers say if I asked what your behaviour was like in the classroom?

A. I really think they would say pretty good, especially in the last two years. Once I was working for my exams I really started paying attention and I hardly ever missed school. I think I've grown up a lot in the last year or two.

Q. You've got quite good A level results, why have you decided to apply to us now rather than go to university and apply for our graduate training scheme?

A. I did think about university, but I know I want to join the Police Force and I really want to learn on the job. I know I would be a bit older if I joined after university, but your training looks very thorough and I want to learn about real situations as quickly as possible.

Regardless of the level to which you took your education, employers will look at how it has contributed to your choice of career and your career progression and what skills it has given you that you can use effectively in the workplace. Questions around these two themes will underpin much of what you are asked about your education when you are being interviewed.

Tip

Don't be daunted, remember that none of these questions means the interviewer thinks you have made a bad or wrong decision, they simply want to check that you have looked at the options available and weighed up the pros and cons carefully. They are looking at your attitude to taking responsible decisions that affect a major area of your life. They need some reassurance that you are not going to change your mind a few weeks after you have started the job.

The brief questionnaire below will help you focus on some the qualities that your education has helped you develop.

Score the items below from 1 to 5 to assess which qualities your education has helped you develop.

Slight extent	1	2	3	4	5	Great extent

Personal development	Score
1. Ability to learn from your own experience.	
2. Ability to reflect on your experiences.	
3. Ability to take decisions.	
4. Ability to research information.	
5. Ability to form concepts.	
6. Ability to learn something new.	
7. Ability to assess your own strengths and weaknesses.	
8. Ability to meet deadlines.	
9. Ability to organize information.	
10. Ability to plan for the future.	

Familiarity with your education should become second nature to you before you begin discussing it at job interviews.

Final tips on reviewing and promoting your education

1. If you already have examination results, make sure you know what they are.

2. Make sure you can find your certificates. These are not often requested, but it is annoying if they are and then you can't find them.

3. If you are still awaiting results, give a reasonably accurate, but optimistic prediction of what you expect to achieve.

4. Talk to the teacher, tutor or lecturer or trainer who you would like to use as your academic or educational referee. If you let them know in advance, they are more likely to say nice things about you and to be able to put more thought into what they say.

5. Use the questionnaire in this chapter to organize your responses.

Chapter three

all
work

making your employment
history work for you

Your employment history may consist of anything from a Saturday job you held while still at school to 20 or more years' experience in professional, technical or managerial work in your chosen field. Wherever you are upon this spectrum, your employment history to date is of great interest to your prospective employer. They will want to know how it fits in with your overall career and ambitions, what you have done that may be of direct relevance to the post you are now seeking, what you have learned about your work styles through your previous jobs. They will be looking for evidence of a continual path of development, even though this may include some changes of direction and some sideways rather than upwards moves. They will want to know what you are like as a colleague, whether you can contribute ideas or motivate others, see projects through, cope with pressure and much, much more.

Which qualities and characteristics they are most interested in will clearly vary according to the type of work you are seeking. The level of expectations they will have is to some extent dictated by how much experience you have had so far. Whatever the situation, they will expect you to be able to give clear and cogent answers about all aspects of your work experience. Chapter 8 later in this book will deal specifically with some of the possible problem areas in your career history such as losing a job or having a very patchy work record. This chapter will focus on common questions likely to be faced by most candidates.

The questions and answers in this chapter draw on examples of candidates who have had very little work experience and those who already have a substantial career behind them. Consider the questions and answers which best reflect your circumstances.

Q. **I see that you have had a Saturday job at your local chemist while you were studying for your GCSEs. What did you learn from this job?**

A. I found it quite exciting because it was the first job I had ever had. I really enjoyed talking to customers and I had a really helpful manager who took time to explain things about stock control and ordering and all that side of things. I ended up helping with the training when we took on new Saturday staff and I got some extra days there during my school holidays.

Q. **I see you took on a part-time job doing data entry while you were a student. How useful was this?**

A. It was the final year of my course, so I did not want to take on something that was too intellectually challenging and I did need the money. Actually it taught me a great deal about being thorough and being able to cope with repetition when you have to. I was made supervisor for some shifts and I got on really well with other staff and saw how important it is for a team under pressure to work well together. My knowledge of IT meant I could do a little bit of trouble shooting for them too and that was really satisfying.

Q. **I see that your business studies course included one year's work experience, what are the three most significant things you learned from that year?**

A. I was delighted to get a placement in the customer relations department of such a large telecommunications company and it really taught me so many things, but the most significant three were how to work as part of a team, to ask the right questions so that I could become effective quickly and above all, common sense. You can never predict exactly what form an enquiry will take and you don't always have a standard reply, so you have to think on your feet and come up with something sensible.

Q. **You have applied for a permanent position with us, but I see that you have been doing temporary jobs for several different employers over the past three years. Why is that?**

(The interviewer wants to know whether you have got what it takes to hold down a permanent job.)

A. Since deciding to go into hotel management I have always liked the idea of working for an independent operator rather than one of the major chains, so I decided to get as much valuable experience as I could in all aspects of hotel work, while I waited for the right opportunity to come along. As you can see, many of my temporary jobs have been with the major chains and I have learned a lot, but it has confirmed that I do want to work somewhere where there is more scope for individual flair and some very traditional values of old-fashioned customer service too.

A. My main reason for temping was that I had not made a really definite decision — I thought I could gain experience of different work environments and the different types of administrative work within various organizations. The experience was really useful and has shown me that I much prefer to work for a smaller company like yours, where I feel far more involved and understand several aspects of your work and your customers. I like being part of a busy team and it brings out the best in me.

Q. **Since completing your course at university you seem to have done mainly bar work and other routine catering jobs. How do you think these are going to help you as a trainee in our IT department?**

A. The main reason I took those jobs was because I have been studying part time for a master's course in business information technology and I really wanted to do well in this, as my first degree in American studies isn't so vocational. I have had lot of contact with employers carrying out information interviews for my course project which has got me in touch with your business. Actually the catering and bar jobs were useful, you learn so much about customers, about solving problems and about thinking on your feet.

Q. **Your CV shows that you have done a lot of voluntary work, but not much paid employment. Why is that?**

(This question leaves you wondering whether they are asking you to outline the benefits of your voluntary experience and relate them to this current application, or suggesting you only work when you feel like it — concentrate on the first option.)

A. My voluntary work has been very varied, working in a hospital, for a local community youth group and on an environmental project. At one time I was working on all three at once and ended up with a 50-hour working week. I have learned so much about working in teams, negotiating and being well organized, but above all, it was the fund raising for these projects that enabled me to clarify that it was in fund raising, promotional work and marketing that I could see my future career.

Q. **You have only been with your current employer for 18 months — why have you decided to make a move now?**

A. I took the job because I have an overall interest in product design and it was a really good start for me, even though I had never thought much about lawnmowers before. I had always wanted to get into the motor vehicle industry because rebuilding old cars is a real passion of mine. When I saw that you were advertising I knew it was an opportunity not to be missed and I have learned a lot working with the design team for the last 18 months.

Q. **You have been with your current employer for 22 years, what has made you decide to apply elsewhere now?**

A. That 22 years may have been with one company, but the company has grown and my role within it has changed several times and I have had several promotions while working there. I started off in their accounts department with a manual accounting system and now I am deputy head of purchasing and took responsibility for installing our latest electronic purchasing system. I like the company and I respect the way they work, but I am certainly ready and qualified to take on a job as head of purchasing and I could bring a great deal of experience to your company. I could go on to outline some of my particular skills if you wish.

A. It sounds a long time when you put it like that and I suppose 22 years in a Government department *is* a long time, but my work has been varied and I now manage a department of more than 100 staff. My experience in policy development and as a policy adviser puts me in an ideal position to take on this position with you. My experience in the Civil Service has helped me become very resilient, very thorough and good at interpreting complex information. I am sure I could use these skills very effectively for you.

Tip

Don't be ruffled by questions that seem to imply that you have been somewhere too long, not long enough, etc. With answers like those above, you can put your interviewer's mind at rest and sell yourself effectively too.

Q. You ran your own business for three years — how do you feel you will fit into a situation where you won't have total responsibility for all the decisions, where work will be delegated to you by somebody else?

A. It was exciting running my own catering business and it went well, I built up a substantial base of satisfied customers, but it became more and more difficult to compete with new legislation and I think even more significantly, I actually missed working with other people. I worked for catering companies before I ran my business and when I left I was still enjoying it, I like working in teams and as this is a management job I shall have considerable responsibility I am sure.

Tip

Expect questions that focus on your performance at work, your successes, failures, satisfactions, difficulties and attitudes to colleagues.

Q. What would your current manager say about your work?

A. She would say I was a very committed and enthusiastic member of the department. I believe she would mention in particular that I keep calm when there is a lot of pressure and that I don't let attention to detail slip when we are close to a deadline.

Tip

If you sound too wonderful, they may come back at you, so be ready to justify your answer or give further information.

Q. That all sounds very promising, but if she was then asked to come up with any faults or weaknesses what might she say?

A. She might say that I sometimes get involved in too many projects at once — that I can get a little bit carried away with enthusiasm and I have to discipline myself to curb that and be even more willing to delegate some projects to others. I have become much more effective at delegation during the past 18 months.

Q. You have been in management for five years now, what might staff who are managed by you say if they were asked to appraise you?

A. I have a great relationship with my staff and I am sure they would pick out the fact that I always try to listen to people's ideas and suggestions regardless of their position within the department. They would say I encourage them to take individual responsibility, but that I am approachable (usually) if they are running into any problems.

Your answer might provoke a follow-up question (or even the need to reach for an airline sickbag.)

Q. Would they all be that positive — there must be aspects of your management style that some of them would be less enthusiastic about?

A. I'm not sure that it's my style they sometimes find difficult — I have had to implement some unpopular decisions, for example, introducing evening work rosters that were completely new to our department and that upset a lot of staff and caused genuine problems for many of them. I think that offering people a full and truthful explanation about why the decision had been made and trying to offer some flexibility in implementing it helped staff to accept the situation, but there are some who are still annoyed about it.

Q. You say your staff like you and you all get on well as a team, does this mean you are a bit of a pushover?

(Be prepared for nasty questions like this that may be sprung on you.)

A. No, there is a world of difference between involving staff in consultation and communicating effectively with them and allowing people to take liberties. My section has one the best records in the organization for low absentee rates and time keeping, and attitudes to taking on extra work are very healthy.

Q. If you have had a recent performance appraisal, what has it highlighted as work goals for the coming year?

A. Yes, we do have an annual performance appraisal; my most recent one was done four months ago. The main point that came up was that I was ready to take on greater management responsibility and also more responsibility for training new staff. As a follow-up to the appraisal, I have already attended one course on effective management styles and another on dealing with staff disciplinary issues.

Q. Have you ever found yourself in a position where you don't get on with a colleague and how have you tackled this?

A. Yes, in the job prior to my current one I really didn't hit it off with our head of public relations; we were both on the same level, so neither of us could pull rank to solve the problem. In the end I grasped the nettle and persuaded him that we should have a talk and try to work out an effective strategy for us to work together — we really needed to with me working in marketing. We had a pretty frank discussion and although I can't say we ended up the best of friends, we did gain more respect for one another's roles and we certainly worked more productively together. I was really glad I had taken the initiative.

Q. If we asked a colleague of yours to describe a fault you have, what would they come up with?

A. My last manager might say I was sometimes a little too impatient with other staff. I find it very frustrating when people don't do their bit, especially if we are trying to meet a deadline. I have learned that taking a bit of time to explain why things must be done now and also reminding people of their obligations to the team does pay off and I get a better response by working in that way, so I have learned a lot about how to get the best out of people and benefited from feeling far less stressed myself.

Q. How do you cope under pressure? This is a very busy department you have applied to join.

A. I enjoy a certain amount of pressure — it makes me alert and very motivated. There are limits and I try to avoid pressure becoming too great by planning my workload well ahead, but sometimes the unexpected crops up however well you plan. In my current job as production editor I can have everything ready for the magazine deadline and a client suddenly decides they want to change an advert or a picture — I have to decide whether it's realistically possible to do this without making the magazine late and if it isn't, I have to keep calm and try to ensure that we don't lose the client — that is always a very pressured situation.

A. I have worked in social services for eight years now and every department I have worked for has been busy and I have managed a heavy caseload. It is stressful when you are dealing with several difficult cases at once, but I find the most useful way of coping is to talk to colleagues and managers to gain some support and also to learn to switch off and leave work behind when I leave the office. I used to find that difficult, but I find that going for a swim at the end of the day and also doing an evening class in something completely different to the job — I am doing a course in Italian at present — really helps me to switch off and be more effective again the next morning.

A. Marking examination papers is always one of the most pressured times of year because I have to do it thoroughly and yet there is an absolute deadline. I cope by developing a really clear routine for my marking and by keeping the rest of my life very simple during those weeks. Of course that's a kind of planned pressure; there's also the unexpected pressure, such as when staff suddenly go off sick or leave and I have to plan all the extra cover for the department and inevitably put pressure on others. Involving people and remembering to thank them helps to soften the blow.

Q. How do you cope if a project you are working on goes wrong?

A. First, I assess the steps we need to take to optimize damage limitation and deal with the immediate problem. Once the crisis is over, I analyze what went wrong and I include colleagues in this discussion, so that we can pinpoint how we might avoid the same thing happening again.

Tip

Don't always reveal a weakness or a mistake.

Nightmare to avoid

A highly qualified overseas development manager was on his way to an interview for a prestigious post. He got to the interview late because he drove his Mercedes into the back of a lorry. He telephoned for assistance and managed not to be quite as late as the chair of the interview panel who apologized but said he had been stuck behind some twit who had driven his car into the back of a lorry and what a pity such people were allowed on the roads. The interviewee chose not to disclose the story.

Perfection is impossible and interviewers know this, but they do want to ascertain that you are capable, confident and willing to do the job. They want that understandable reassurance that they are not about to employ someone with psychopathic tendencies or take on an accountant who will disappear with the company's funds within three months of taking up work. Clearly, if this is your intention you won't announce it at your interview, but your prospective employer will try through both interviews and perhaps, psychological tests too, to ensure that you are a reasonable human being.

Tip

Consider carefully which weaknesses you choose to reveal when you are asked about these at interview. "I don't have any at all" is a reply that lacks conviction and immediately lets slip that either arrogance or dishonesty may be among your less pleasing personal qualities. If, however, you believe you may be harbouring psychopathic tendencies or you absconded with the tea club funds from your last job, this may be a truth better kept to yourself. Consider those weaknesses which can be seen as training needs as areas that may require some development, but you have already begun to work on successfully or, those weaknesses which can be made to sound like strengths impatient/enthusiastic about doing a good job, take on too many projects/really hard worker, etc.

All the questions about your work experience link to the fundamental questions mentioned in Chapter 1, can you do the job, will you do the job and will you fit in.

Think about which of the following words might describe your working style and these will help you construct some of your own answers.

Discerning	Receptive	Assessing	Observing
Productive	Reflecting	Risk taking	Careful
Practical	Questioning	Active	Responsible
Co-operative	Analytical	Decisive	Supportive
Creative	Thorough	Measured	Dynamic
Efficient	Independent	Imaginative	Committed

Tip

Remember that if you are going to use any of these words in your answers, you must be able to back up your claims with actual situations, problems or challenges.

Q. **Tell me how your experience to date makes you suitable for this job.**

A. I started as a junior reporter on the local paper I am working for now and it was an excellent way to learn the basic skills of chasing stories, interviewing, writing and following stories up. Education became quite an issue in our area because of various school closures and mergers and that gave me a chance to get really involved in an issue and build up a network of useful contacts and be well informed. I know all of this would be relevant to a national daily like yours, I feel ready to make the move, it is something I have always wanted and my current editor has been really encouraging, even though he says he does not want to lose me.

A. Among the many things I have learned from my time as a store manager, I have learned a great deal about our fashion product range, what sells well and items that you think will be great, but just don't seem to have that vital appeal to customers. I enjoy many aspects of management especially anything connected with display and merchandising and I think I would contribute really well to the buying department. I think I have a real feel for what customers want and a realistic approach to cost.

A. I have been a nurse at this hospital for six years now and since I also have a degree, I am in an ideal position to take advantage of your management training scheme. I love working with patients, but I suppose one of my greatest satisfactions is training and supporting new staff on the ward and helping them to understand how their contribution is essential to both efficiency and high standards of patient care. I would like the opportunity to take this part of my work further and the management scheme would certainly allow me to do this. I think it pays dividends to have some managers who have come up through the grass roots of nursing.

Q. What would you say is your greatest strength?

A. I am sure it is dealing with people — my interpersonal skills are very good. I seem to be able to pitch myself at just the right level, whether I am presenting something to the management board or solving a problem with a customer on the telephone. I am good at persuading people around to my point of view without bullying them. I always enjoyed debates and discussions at university and I have become a good negotiator.

A. I am really good at spotting ways in which a process can be carried out more efficiently to save time and money. I managed to cut back the number of procedures involved in our internal ordering system in my current job and at first colleagues said it wouldn't work, but it is going really well now.

Q. What is your time management like? How do you plan your working week, for example?

A. At the end of the week I make a list the most important tasks that lay ahead for the following week and decide which ones I shall tackle first. I usually organize a brief team meeting first thing on a Monday morning, so that anyone can bring up anything they are concerned about or where they feel there are likely to be real pressure points during the week.

Q. How do you set about prioritizing your work load?

A. Perhaps I should give you an example. As head of a department in a large recruitment consultancy, a great deal of post is addressed to me and although it is partly sorted by other staff I still face a full in-tray every morning. I quickly sort everything into three piles, things that need to be followed up straight away, for instance vacancies to be processed or new clients to be followed up. I have a second file of relatively important items, invitations to conferences, internal memos, etc, and a third heap that may well be destined for the rubbish bin — irrelevant product adverts and endless questionnaires.

Q. What action do you take if you have members of staff working for you who really don't get on with one another, to the point where this is affecting other staff?

A. Of course I do make my own assessment of where faults might lie, but I get those staff together in a meeting and give them an opportunity to raise what they find difficult about their colleague, without allowing blatant insults and then I ask them to suggest things which would make the situation work better. Of course, this is assuming they are both good employees and that there are faults on both sides. If it is simply a case of one person behaving unreasonably, then I would outline my dissatisfactions and ask them to make some improvements.

Q. What sort of contribution do you make to a team or work group?

A. Having graduated last year, I am fairly new to work teams, but I took part in two group projects while on my engineering course. On one project I was been asked to lead and I found it quite a challenge motivating other team members so that they all pulled their weight. I learned how vital it is for people to really understand their specific tasks and to realize how these relate to the whole project. In my second group project, I had specific responsibility for industrial liaison, gathering data from employers and working closely with them. I got a lot out of this, but I preferred the role of team leader.

Q. **What is the most difficult situation you have had to deal with at work and how successful were you in dealing with it?**

A. When I was working as head of finance in an educational organization, I had to implement a three per cent cut in our annual budget across all departments and it was my task to work out how this cut should be shared across all departments, whether some should bear greater or smaller reductions, rather than simply implementing a blanket cut. It was hard because I was new, it was an unpopular policy and everyone was trying hard to convince me that they should be spared from the burden of the cuts. I kept a clear head, undertook a thorough analysis of the previous year's cuts and potential income-generating activities in each department and I ensured that my decision was transparent and understood by everyone. I was not popular with all departments, but our finances improved in the following year, which really vindicated my actions.

Q. **What is the most satisfying aspect of your current job?**

A. I continue to enjoy dealing with patients and their families, but I think over the past two years developing induction and training programmes for new members of staff has given me the greatest satisfaction and enjoyment. It seems to me that if staff get good training and support from the minute they join us, then patient care will be of a higher standard and those staff will, in turn, get much more from their work.

A. Managing to get a really major client on board to advertise with us has been a real thrill. We had tried several times in the past and they had always eluded us, but I must have put together just the right package and offered them the right price, because they are now a major source of income for us and the relationship with them is going really well.

Q. Is there anything you don't like about your current job?

A. I have to confess that I don't like some of the routine paper work, especially since in my opinion, a lot of it could be replaced with an on-screen system. I have developed the attitude of getting it done quickly, so that it doesn't pile up or get behind and that's the way I've tried to make it more palatable, even if I can't say it's exactly exciting.

Q. Describe a situation where you have had to deal with an angry customer/client/member of the public. How did you cope and what was the outcome?

A. You do get angry customers in restaurants and on one occasion a regular customer who often brought business clients for lunch suddenly went really wild complaining that their wine was off and that they had had to wait for too long for their meal. He was really shouting and everyone stopped eating and looked round. It was the manager's day off so I had to deal with him. I kept very calm, spoke quietly and immediately offered them another bottle of wine. I apologized for the delay and explained that it was because all the meals were freshly prepared and that a soufflé always took a few extra minutes. I think he was just having a bad day because he calmed down pretty quickly.

A. My last company built some specialist software for a client to handle its database. The client kept altering their requirements and as a result we had not got the system up and running for them by the agreed date. As the sales consultant who'd dealt with them to begin with, it fell to me to placate them and it was not easy. I think being prepared to apologize straight away helped and I also arranged a deal where we offered some additional systems support — a little more than had been agreed in the original contract. Of course, I got clearance to do this from my managing director.

A.   A father became really angry and abusive at a parents' evening once because his daughter had not had a very good school report — I was her class teacher at the time. She was a disruptive pupil and she had not done very well, although I had tried to give her attention and support. It was very unpleasant, but I tried to get him talking about the things she was better at and why they were working well and what she enjoyed at home and as soon as we got into a proper conversation where he realized I knew who his daughter was and she wasn't just a number or a box to be ticked, then things calmed down pretty quickly. He became more involved in her schooling after that.

Of course, not every awkward encounter in your working history will have had such successful and happy outcomes as these three, but what the interviewer wants to know is how you dealt with the situation, what strategies and tactics you employed to try to bring about a good result, even if, sometimes, it does not work.

All the questions and answers in this chapter will vary according to the job you are applying for. If you are being interviewed for a position as somebody's personal assistant then alarm bells will ring if you announce that you feel you are a natural leader and like to take firm control of situations. If you are being interviewed to lead a project or head up a department, then by all means stress your skills of listening, involving other people in the decision process and being aware of other people's strengths, but ultimately you are there to lead, to motivate and to take responsibility for ensuring that the job is done on time or that your department runs smoothly and effectively.

The key to answering many of these questions successfully is in being able to illustrate your answers with accounts of situations taken from your past and current work. If you say you cope well working under pressure, give an example of when you have done this. If you say you are an effective team leader, you should describe a team you have led and how you were effective. Never assume that the interviewer knows any of this — they may be skilled, but they are not telepathic.

A constructive way to plan your answers to these questions is to look at your employment history and list some of the most valuable learning points from each job you have held.

The following chart will help you organize this information and become familiar with it.

Employment	What I learned	What I achieved	What I found difficult

Questions aren't always asked in neat categories relating to education, employment history, etc but it is a useful way to organize your responses.

Final tips to make your employment work for you

1. Check your CV or application form to remind yourself of exactly what your employment history comprizes.

2. Don't discount experiences such as voluntary work or brief periods of work experience — this is especially important if you only have a brief job history so far.

3. If you have helpful colleagues, friends or managers, talk to them about your faults and your strengths to clarify the picture for yourself. You may discover good points you weren't even aware of and, if you discover any bad ones, you don't need to share these at an interview.

4. Spend much more time thinking about your strengths and successes than your flaws and failures.

5. Ensure that you use a range of situations to demonstrate your selling points; don't build all your answers around one project or one incident.

Chapter four

your kind of company

what you need to know and how to let them know you know

It is hardly surprising that employers want to know why you have targeted them with your application. Anyway, you have told them a lot about you, through your application, so why shouldn't you have some valuable information too? In reality, you may be making multiple applications, especially if you are really keen on a change of job or career or if you have just completed your education or professional training. Yet every employer wants to feel that they have been chosen and specially selected by you. They know that you are probably shopping around, but you still need those convincing arguments and that winning flattery at hand. Careful thought and intelligent research will prepare you to answer all their likely questions on this topic.

Tip

Whatever type of work you are pursuing, carry out as much research as you can before you go to the interview. In this way, you are well informed, you can answer those questions which are designed to find out how much effort you have put in before the interview and you are better prepared to get any questions that you may have answered at your interview. This necessity for research is not restricted to the world of large, commercial organizations.

Multi-nationals, small IT companies, schools, health care trusts or your local corner shop — they all merit some investigation. Remind yourself of the information resources available to you to help your information gathering:

- company brochures
- annual reports
- company websites
- local and national press
- trade press
- business directories
- business and other reference libraries
- Job Centres
- recruitment agencies
- university careers libraries
- professional and trade organizations
- other people who work for the organization or do similar work to that which you are applying for
- your own direct experience of using the company's products or services.

In fact, all the resources that you have already been using as part of your job search.

Before considering the following questions and answers, be very clear about why the interviewer is asking them. They want to know whether you have put any effort into finding out about them — whether you really have considered carefully the kind of organization they are — their products, their status, their image, etc. They are not seeking evidence about just how much information you can remember — a few intelligent thoughts and comments will go much further than being able to quote large chunks of last year's annual report from memory.

Q. What do you think of our company/organization?

A. As a major clearing bank, I have been aware of your existence for a long time. I really liked your recent advertising campaign, and being an internet enthusiast I was impressed that you were one of the first to set up internet banking facilities. It was the main reason I chose to change my bank, so I have experience from both sides of the fence — from being one of your customers.

A. I had already decided that I wanted to teach in an inner city school. It helped that you were happy to allow me an informal visit before I put in my application and I thought there was a really happy atmosphere in all the classrooms I visited. I am keen to work in a school which involves parents and the local community and your recent fund raising concert demonstrated that very clearly. It was really enjoyable too, I was part of the audience and it's great to see music being given a high priority.

A. I have often popped in here for a coffee and a sandwich. The place has always been bright and clean and the staff here seem friendly and efficient. I like the range of food you offer and the fact that you seem to be on really good terms with so many of your customers.

A. I began to notice your products advertised frequently in 'Software Today' and I started to sit up and take notice. The fact that you seem to put so much energy into designing specialist software for individual clients really interests me — I like the idea of using my technical skills to work closely with customers.

A. Your website is really informative and has shown me a great deal about your products and your proposed future developments. I am very excited by the idea of working for a smaller company where my ideas can make a real contribution.

Tip

Notice how all the answers above, though geared to different employers, have two things in common. First, they demonstrate that candidates have thought about who they are applying to within a particular job market and second, each candidate took the opportunity to throw in a positive comment to highlight either their suitability or their enthusiasm for the organization or the position on offer. Ask yourself, could you do this at your next interview?

Nightmare to avoid

"I have read your last three annual reports cover to cover and I wonder if you would like me to quote the annual turnover for those three years for both your widgets and thingies departments separately or possibly as an aggregate figure, of perhaps........" the interviewers will probably be fast asleep by now and on the whole, interviewers should not be bored into submission.

Q. Tell me what you know about this organization.

A. I did a three-week placement in your accounts department and that gave me a lot of contact with all your internal departments and was really informative about what projects you have underway at the moment. It also meant I found out a lot about who your customers are and although my real interest is in marketing, it was a really valuable experience.

A. When I started looking for work with housing associations I arranged informal visits with those who were willing to allow this. Your colleagues were really helpful in arranging a visit for me, not just to your head office but to two of your projects, one for older people and one for single parent families. The projects seemed to be working really well and staff at your main office are incredibly committed to what they are doing — I found that encouraging and quite inspiring — very much the kind of team with whom I'd like to work.

A. I read your entry in 'Advertising World Annual Directory' and noticed that for a comparatively small firm, you deal with an interesting range of clients. I visited your website and found out more about some of your campaigns for small charities and pressure groups. I could say more about what caught my attention about those campaigns if you would like me to.

These are all quite different answers, but all making it clear to the interviewer that the candidate has made a positive choice about this organization and has carried out some appropriate research to support their decision.

Tip

If you find that sometimes, whatever the topic, you are heading for a potentially lengthy answer, it is a good idea to draw breath and check with the interviewer that they would like you to say more. If they decline your offer, don't feel crest fallen and foolish, you may already have said enough to convince them, or they may have specific questions they wish to ask you later that further explore the topic you have been covering.

Q. Are you familiar with any of our products/services/projects?

A. Yes several, but particularly your microwave meals and your soft drinks range, I'm a real fan of some of your flavoured mineral waters. Since I started taking an interest in your company I have taken note of where your products are placed on supermarket shelves and observed which groups of customers seem drawn to them. I could say a little more if you wish.

A. I first found out about your local youth theatre projects during our local arts week last Summer when I saw your production of 'Blood Wedding'. I was interested in arts and theatre administration then, so I took the opportunity to talk to some of the cast and some of the staff back stage. Since then I've followed up on several of your community projects.

A. At present I am not as familiar with your product range as I would like to be, but I am quick at assimilating knowledge and information and I would certainly enjoy learning more about all the products you currently supply.

This last answer is not ideal, but it is better then making something up because if you do say something bland like "yes, I think all your products are excellent" you are likely to be asked something like "What do you think is so good about them?" or "Which one do you like best then?" and you are going to feel unbelievably foolish if you have to say you don't know.

Q. How would you rate us against our competitors?

A. I certainly think you're the best of the three free newspapers that are delivered round here. You all have to make money from advertising and yet you manage to include far more interesting editorial and many more stories that really do concern local issues — I think that makes a real difference.

A. Well, once I had decided I wanted to get into management in the fast food industry I looked at several of the major players and considered their products, their premises, their customer groups and their business performance. Compared to the other pizza chains I think your outlets look really clean and bright, the service is friendly and you do seem to try to preserve a slightly more authentic Italian feel and that really appeals to me.

Q. If you had a free hand, how would you like to see us develop over the next three years?

A. I know that you are already investing heavily in research and development and I would certainly continue to develop that emphasis. I would like to see you develop further into some of the European markets where Germany and Italy seem to have quite a strong grip at the moment — perhaps we should have more European satellite offices.

A. The growing market for organic and environmentally friendly products is very significant I believe and it is not an area that your company has touched on all that much so far. I would like to investigate the production costs and the feasibility of developing some of these — I am sure that market will grow significantly over the next few years.

Q. What do you think is the most interesting aspect of our work?

A. I am very interested in your African development. My father worked in Africa for a while when I was in my early teens and I have a real feeling for the place and of course it is a really interesting new market too.

A. I have read several articles in the press about your recent projects in inner cities working with homeless families. The projects looked really innovative and this was a subject I researched and wrote about for my final year dissertation at university. I'd be really interested to see how those projects work in the longer term and I would love to be involved with that kind of work.

A. So many city law firms seem to concentrate only on commercial clients, but you have departments dealing with a whole range of different aspects of the law. My particular interest in environmental law makes you an obvious choice for me and you have been involved in some really high profile cases in that area.

Nightmare to avoid

Don't make assumptions about the kind of organization you are applying to. One candidate unwisely told the interview panel that he had applied for the job because he was tired and he thought things might be fairly easy going and he could have a bit of a rest. In fact, it was a busy education department that had just undergone staff cuts and significantly increased workloads.

Q. What do you think of our company website?

A. I think it is excellent, it's easy to locate the information you want and very informative. If it were up to me, I might be inclined to include a few more photographs.

Q. What do you think of our graduate recruitment brochure?

A. I thought the most useful part was the series of profiles of recent graduates, outlining their background and their career development within the company. I would like to have seen one or two more profiles from the technical side, which would have been especially helpful for me since I am applying for R and D. Leaving aside this minor criticism, I have looked at several graduate brochures over the past few months and yours is certainly one of the most informative.

Tip

Interviewers are not looking simply to be flattered — they want an intelligent response. Of course this does not mean they want to hear that the best use for their brochure is to line the cat's litter tray or that your granny could do a better job of their website.

Q.   What advantages do you think we have in the market place?

A.   You have a smaller range of products than some of your competitors, but those products have a deserved reputation for being of a high quality and your advertising and promotion campaigns mean that consumers are well aware of these products. I am sure it has been cost effective for you to gear your production in this direction and last year's figures certainly bear that out.

A.   Living in the town, I know exactly which other restaurants around here are your main competitors and I must confess to having eaten at all of them at one time or another. It says a great deal that you always have to book up here at least two weeks ahead for a Friday and Saturday night and it goes without saying that I think the cuisine is wonderful — really interesting with plenty of use of fresh local produce — that is one of the many reasons I have applied to be your assistant chef.

Q.   How do you think we can remain successful?

A.   You already have a strong client base and it is important to keep those clients very happy so that they return to you for their business. Good follow-up service is a real key here. Of course, you want to extend that client base too and effective marketing is important, but then you need to continue to ensure that every aspect of the business backs up those sales and marketing promises. Every employee has their part to play in this, I believe.

Q.   Is there anything you think we do badly?

A.   I'd like to turn that round and look at anything that you might do better, since I am sure you wouldn't enjoy your current success if you were doing anything really wrong. I am surprised that I don't see your products mentioned more frequently in some of the trade press. I know you have a strong customer base, but it can never be a bad thing to extend that.

A. I certainly wouldn't say 'badly' — I wouldn't be applying to join you if I had too many concerns in that direction. I have been a customer of yours in the past and I have sometimes found staff dealing with telephone calls unable to help me, or unsure who to refer me to, which makes me want to look at some of your staff training procedures. You provide a good service and it is important to let potential customers have the information they need with the minimum of difficulty.

Genuine and thoughtful criticism is acceptable — after all, your ideas and input may be about to contribute to the company's success. Be sensitive, saying everything they do and have ever done is wonderful does not show any insight into them, their business, their clients and their market place. On the other hand, no interviewer wants to be told that the organization he or she is working for is out of date, disorganized had poor industrial relations and is generally hopeless. Your answers need to demonstrate that you have thought carefully about the organization you are applying to, undertaken what information gathering you reasonably can and applied that to come up with some cogent answers and suggest you brain would be an asset to them.

How much research you can realistically be expected to carry out before an interview does vary according to the kind of organization you are seeking to join. A large business is likely to produce reports and brochures and to have a website, whereas a very small enterprise may not offer very much in the way of tangible information. Interview candidates are often reluctant to approach organizations to see what information is available. They imagine it displays some sort of weakness not to have been able to locate such information from some other mysterious resource. The contrary is the case; no-one is going to lose marks for using initiative and a company is often very happy to send information they have or, on some occasions, to allow you to have an informal discussion with someone on the telephone or through a visit, before you attend your formal interview. There is never any harm in asking. The very worst that can happen is that you can be told "no".

Run through the list of possible resources mentioned at the beginning of this chapter to check which may be useful for you.

You may find it helpful to see which of the following questions you can answer once you have carried out your research.

1. What basic facts do you know about the company, its size, its location, etc?
2. What do you know about its products/services?
3. Do you know how successful it has been over the past one to three years?
4. Are you aware of who its most significant competitors are?
5. Do you know how well it is performing measured against its most significant competitors?
6. What have you been able to find out about its internal structures? What kind of management models does it favour? What is its record on industrial relations?
7. Are you aware of the ways in which it markets itself? How successful is it at conveying a particular image of itself?
8. Have you encountered any negative publicity or information about this organization?
9. Are you aware of any future developments, projects, etc, that it has planned?
10. Is there anything you can suggest that would make it more effective, more efficient or more successful?

You may want to add questions of your own and some of the above questions will not be appropriate if you are applying to some types of organization. For example, while it is easy to find large quantities of information about the Civil Service or a multi-national company, information may be more limited in the case of a local small business or a project funded by a charity. Nevertheless, it is a useful discipline to see just how much you do know about your prospective employer.

Your kind of company, but are you their kind of person?

Many of the questions in the first half of this chapter focus on what you know about the organization you are hoping to join. If you are on the ball and, as your interview technique becomes better and better, you will be able to weave some personal selling points into the answers you give to those questions — in exactly the way that the model answers demonstrate. You will, however, also find yourself being asked quite similar sounding questions, but questions where the focus is much more on you and why *you* believe this particular employer is suitable for you.

Q. Why do you want to work for us?

A. I had an open mind at the beginning of my final year at university, apart from knowing that I wanted to join a large corporation with a good reputation and I was simply looking at a whole range of recruitment information and websites. One of the things that stood out about you was the flexibility you offer in offering new staff training in several areas before they are definitely committed to one area.

Q. Who else are you applying to?

A. All the other leading firms of accountants, but I would far rather work for you if I had the choice. I attended one of your recruitment events and had a chance to talk to staff who you have taken on recently and I am really impressed with the support you give for professional training and qualifying. Even more important to me though, is knowing you have such a large and successful computer auditing department, that is something which really interests me and would really bring my IT skills and my interest in accounting together.

A. I have really applied to anything that might help me get my foot in the door because anything to do with arts and theatre is so competitive that I don't think I ought to be too choosy — I accept I will have to work my way up. That's not to say I am not a very strong applicant, I have helped out voluntarily with our last two local arts weeks and of course, there's the box office job I had last summer at the Wild Side Theatre. I am really interested in this administrative job you are offering, my experience to date suits it very well.

A. No, I have drawn up a list of other companies that would interest me and I have my CVs all ready to go, but after having had a part-time job with you for a while last year, I felt I would really like to work for you and although it is taking a bit of a risk, I would see how things went with my application to you, before I send off any more CVs.

Q. Have you received job offers from anyone else?

A. No, not so far, although I do have another interview to go to on Friday.

A. Yes, I have just received an offer from Spring Fresh Foods to join their product development division, but I am more interested in your product range and I'm also impressed by your record on environmental issues.

Q. If one of our competitors offered you a job now, would you accept?

A. I would have to look very carefully at exactly what they were offering, not simply in terms of financial reward, but how relevant it was to my experience and how it might develop my career, but I would really much prefer to work here if I were given the opportunity.

An interviewer is not going to base his or her decision on whether to make you a job offer on what other applications you have in the pipeline, but examining your job hunting strategy is another way of assessing some of your planning, deciding and analyzing skills. If they are really impressed with you at interview, it will be of interest to them that other people may be making you offers and that they could lose out. Don't take any unwise gambles on this one though, like saying you have had other offers if you haven't, if you are level pegging with another candidate (and this can happen, especially where several staff are being taken on at the same time), they may decide you are a lost cause.

Final tips on finding out as much about them as they find out about you

1. Do your research in advance wherever this is possible.

2. If you really can't do this, make use of the time immediately before your interview either by talking to members of staff or taking note of any publicity about the organization and its customers that you can find.

3. Remember that all this hard work before the interview benefits you too — it helps you work out whether they are the right employers for you, not only whether they think you are suitable for them.

Chapter five

the
personal touch

all about your personality, your
skills and your interests

In Chapter 1, which dealt with being thoroughly prepared for interviews, the key point was made that what employers really want to know about is you, every aspect of you and most particularly what kind of person you are and whether you will fit in to the job for which you are applying. Will you get on with other staff, do you have tantrums when somebody asks you to do something you would rather not, or shout at colleagues or customers if things don't go your way? Only the most unwise interviewee would, of course, admit to any of these faults during a selection interview, even if the odd lapses have crept into their working life. Interviewers often focus many of their questions on trying to discover exactly what makes you tick and whether what you have got will combine effectively and efficiently with the work, the ethos, the direction and the general style of your would-be employer.

Of course, they will glean much of this knowledge from the questions you answer about your current and past employment, your education and the reasons behind your career decisions and career progression, but they may also use some more direct questions to find out more about you.

Q. Tell me something about yourself.

A. Perhaps I should begin by telling you why I have chosen to apply to you for this job at this stage in my career and outline how my experience in my current and previous jobs relates to this post.

A. I'll start by telling you something about the course I have just completed, what I have gained from it and how it links in with my plans for the future.

A. Maybe I should start by telling you one or two of the more unusual things that I have done, what I think I have learned from them and how they would be useful to you if I were to be offered a post here.

(These 'unusual' things could be particular work projects, experiences gleaned from voluntary activities or even leisure interests, so long as you make your answer relevant and interesting.)

A. Well, I could begin by describing the sort of person I think I am, or at least how friends and colleagues would describe me and then I can give you a bit more about my history if that is helpful.

This seemingly simple request to tell an interviewer something about yourself is one of the most forbidding to interviewees and one you would do well to anticipate. The reason it is so difficult is because you are simply unsure of where to begin, what to include, how much to include how long to go on for. You can reasonably assume that your interviewer is not expecting an unexpurgated version of your autobiography beginning with your earliest memory of

Tip

There are two points in your favour with this question. First, it is likely to confront you early in the interview so you will not have used up all your good, potential material as answers to other questions. Second, this is a great opportunity for you to take control, you have carte blanche to elucidate some of the positive points about yourself that you have planned to include in your interview.

when you left your teddy bear in the park and culminating with the dinner party you held last Saturday, but that still does not answer the tricky question of exactly which choice tit-bits to pick out to whet your interviewer's appetite.

The answers suggested above are only openings to what will form part of longer answers that are relevant to you. What they do contain that you should also include is a *clear starting point,* so that the interviewer is aware of what to expect and has the chance to agree that this is okay. It also gives you the opportunity to go on to some other aspects of your life and your personality if you want to. It is perfectly acceptable to give some information and then ask: "Would you like me to say a little more about that?" Or "I could tell you a little more about my career aspirations" Or "I could tell you something about what provides the major satisfactions for me in any job I am doing: In other words, if there is a great deal that you could say, don't indulge in a 15 minute monologue only pausing to check that the interviewer hasn't sloped off for a coffee. Give your answer in discrete chunks, checking at each stage whether they want more.

It may be helpful as part of your interview preparation to ask friends or colleagues how they would describe you — sometimes you become so familiar with yourself, especially if you haven't been asked this type of question for some years, that you find it quite strange to be asked to describe yourself in this way and the opinions of others can be good reminders and hopefully confidence boosters too.

Q. What would you say is your greatest achievement to date?

A. Being asked to manage the department I currently run has been extremely significant for me. I had only been working there for two years and I had assumed that someone with more experience than me would be asked. I had worked hard and put a lot of energy into developing and expanding our customer base. But I had not anticipated a reward coming quite so soon. The real achievement for me is that I have managed to do this and avoid resentment from other staff who might have assumed that they would be asked to do the job.

A. I have to say it has been getting my private airline pilot's licence. I know it is not exactly an everyday skill for this office, but it was an ambition I had held for years, it cost me a lot of money, but it was so exciting when I actually started flying solo and was able to take friends for flights.

A. Achieving a university degree at the age of 37 while bringing up a family of three and holding down a part-time job to help pay the bills. I had not been all that successful academically at school and yet I found I did really well on my course, my results bear that out and it has been worth all the hard work and opened up my career options significantly.

A. To be honest — giving up smoking. I never thought I could do it and I had had dozens of attempts that ended in failure. It isn't just the fact that I don't smoke any more, I have gained so much personal insight and I deal with potentially stressful situations at work so much more effectively now. I feel more energetic, more mentally alert and far calmer now than I ever did before.

Tip

Don't give yourself a hard time by imagining that the candidate being called in after you has just climbed Everest without oxygen, raising £50,000 for charity at the same time, saving an endangered species and still managing to practise the violin every day, to prepare for their debut performance a day after they return. Of course, you might be very unlucky and find yourself competing with such a candidate, but the chances of this are very much in the realms of a lottery win.

What employers like to hear about is something that is not always related to your work situation. Yes, they are interested in your work-related achievements, but they also want to know something about what else you have done that you feel good about. This is not just idle curiosity; your answers may reveal much about what motivates, stimulates and satisfies you.

List any achievements you can think of.

When/where	Achievement	What it meant to me
At work		
At school		
At university/ college		
Through sport		
Through art or music		
Through voluntary work		
Through other leisure activities		
Personal development		

Tip

Don't expect to be able to fill in all the categories, our lives and experiences are all very different, but try to fill in four or five if you can. If you can go for all eight, by all means do.

Q.   What is the most interesting thing you have ever done?

A.   The six months I spent travelling and especially the time I spent in India, was a completely new and different experience for me and made a lasting impression. As well as learning a lot about an entirely different culture and seeing different sights, I learned to be a lot more observant and a lot more personally resourceful.

Q.   What are your three greatest strengths?

A.   Dealing with people, keeping calm when people around me are getting agitated and finding imaginative solutions to problems. Imaginative solutions I have come up with have included using our office space more effectively, I think I have a little bit of a flair for design. I also developed some new motivation courses for junior staff because we were suffering from a rather high staff turnover.

Q.   If we asked a friend of yours to describe your character, what would they say?

A.   I think they would say I am easy to get on with and quite out-going. They would say I have a good sense of humour and am generally cheerful. I think they would also say I am quite good in a crisis — I am often the person who gets telephoned or called on if someone has a problem.

Q.   If we asked a friend of yours to pick out a weakness of yours, what do you think they might say?

A.   I suppose they might say that I can sometimes be a bit impulsive, I get very fired up by a new idea and sometimes a little frustrated if I don't get the chance to carry it through. The plus side of it is that I do have some exciting ideas and many of them do really work.

(Give an example here if this applies to you.)

Q. What would you say is your most significant fault?

A. Getting involved in other people's work. Because I do have considerable experience, colleagues quite often come to me for advice and I am happy to give it, but I have had to learn, and I really have addressed this issue, that it is still their responsibility, I mustn't try to take over. It stems from wanting to be helpful and wanting to see things done well I suppose.

Q. How do you cope with disappointment?

A. Of course, I don't like it, but I have learned to be philosophical. I was really disappointed when I didn't get into my first choice university and yet I ended up enjoying myself and doing well. There is a real difference between disappointments that are beyond your own control and those where you can learn something and try to improve your situation. My disappointment over university made me start applying early to the companies that interested me so that I could avoid a further disappointment.

Sounds very interesting

Applicants for jobs often ask why they should have to spend time on their application forms, CVs and at interviews describing their leisure activities, pastimes and interests. Candidates often worry that they don't have any sporting or outlandish interests (believing that these are the ones of which employers are most likely to approve). Like many others, this is one of those interview topics that gets you wondering what your rival candidates have been up to that could thrill and impress.

Tip

If your favourite pastime is Morris dancing, it is probably best to keep this to yourself. Some interests are best treated as a purely private matter. (Sorry Morris dancers everywhere.)

There are several reasons why interviewers want to know about your interests. If there is something you really enjoy doing and are passionate about, they can experience you at your most enthusiastic and relaxed and find out what you are really like when you are keen on something. It is their hope that this infectious enthusiasm will be a characteristic that you can bring to your job. They may also be trying to find out something about your time management skills — are you able to fit anything else in besides work, study and family? You may have interests that have developed skills that are very beneficial to your work situation. If you have been involved in team sports or other group activities, this will be one way in which you have developed awareness of how groups of people function together. If you are involved in the performing arts you are likely to be confident in a public situation. There are some jobs where having the confidence to take calculated risks is essential and if your interests reflect this thirst for adventure this will be a bonus (provided you don't break your leg a week after joining the company in your drive to become an international snow-boarding champion).

More than all these reasons though, what we choose to do in our free time can speak volumes about what kind of people we are, be that extrovert, sociable, persistent, solitary, creative, energetic, cautious, daring, etc.

Q. You have talked about your current and past jobs and what you got out of education, but you haven't said much about your interests, how do you spend your leisure time?

A. I would certainly say I was a very sociable person, I enjoy company and like entertaining or relaxing with friends. I suppose I have a pretty broad range of interests rather than one over riding passion, but I enjoy music of many different kinds — I play a little bit of guitar, though nothing brilliant. I enjoy reading, especially modern fiction and I take an interest in current affairs, especially those that affect my own local community — for example the plans to close down our local swimming pool.

Q. You say you read a lot of non-fiction as well as fiction, what is the latest non-fiction work you have read and how would you recommend it, or not to others?

A. Jeremy Paxman's *The English*, it was very entertaining, though my main criticism would be that it relied a few too many broad generalizations, I would still recommend it if you haven't read it.

Tip

Just because interests might seem like a 'soft' topic. don't be tempted to lie, your interviewer might really be an avid reader, keen golfer or opera buff, so don't bluff and get caught out.

Q. I see that you play for your local football team, what sort of a player are you?

(They are probably more interested in your team skills than whether you are a crash hot goal scorer.)

A. I usually play at least once a week and I suppose I'm one of the better players. I captain the team when our usual captain is away and I like to encourage young players

Q. I see you are interested in amateur dramatics, do you think that will be useful to you at work?

A. Well it has certainly given me a lot of confidence. I used to worry about public speaking, whereas now I really enjoy it. For instance, when giving presentations to small groups, I find I am quite good at holding my audience's attention and I have learned to use visual aids sparingly, rather than relying on them.

Q. I notice that you are chair of your local tenants' group — how much work does that involve?

A. Apart from monthly meetings which I chair, we are involved in several meetings with the local council and other community groups to work towards improving the quality of life on the estate, less litter, better street lighting, more activities for young people, etc. I was reluctant to take on the chair at first. But it is a role I have really got into now. More than the actual chairing of the meetings I enjoy playing a leading part in some of the negotiations we are undertaking with the local council and we have already had a successful result — the street lighting is much better than it was six months ago.

Tip

Try to use your interests to draw in other information about your personal skills, whether these be in dealing with people, working in teams, organizing events or keeping track of expenditure — these and many more are all useful work skills.

Q. Looking at your CV, your interests appear rather solitary, hill walking, reading, etc. How do you think this reflects your personality?

(Do they suspect you of being a sad and lonely character, incapable of relating to the rest of the human race?)

A. I like to think they suggest a sense of balance. In my current post I spend a lot of time out meeting potential customers and in the office we are a busy team of ten. I enjoy socializing, but it can be good to relax completely sometimes and do something different. In any case, hill walking is something I quite often do in company.

Q. What are your interests outside work?

A. I enjoy reading, music, films, theatre, music, most sports, travel, cooking, gardening and much more.

Tip

Avoid giving a long list of interests with no explanation of any of them and don't list so many that your interviewer is left wondering how you manage to squeeze a working day into this busy life. Karl Marx may have said that the fulfilled human being participates in at least five different meaningful activities every day, but it is a rare employer indeed who relishes an introduction to Marxist theory halfway through a job interview.

Take care not to get carried away when you are talking about something that interests you, it is easy to fall into this trap because for you it is 'safe' territory, but restrict yourself to aspects of your interests which say something about you, rather than giving your interviewer a lecture on the rules of contract bridge or advice on exactly which alpine to plant in their rockery — what is a passion for you could be quite dull for your interviewer.

Consider how your interests describe your personality.

Interest/leisure activity	What it conveys about me

Tip

Whatever activity you are describing and whether it relates to work or leisure, consider the following list of active verbs — try to draw some of them into your answers.

Achieved	Identified	Performed
Analyzed	Implemented	Persuaded
Arranged	Initiated	Planned
Calculated	Interacted	Produced
Communicated	Mediated	Selected
Created	Modified	Simplified
Decided	Motivated	Succeeded
Developed	Negotiated	Tested
Established	Organized	

Don't drive yourself to distraction trying to remember which ones you have included in your answers so far.

The skilled individual

Chapter 3 gave examples of many of the questions you are likely to face relating to your past and current employment and some of these questions asked for particular qualities and skills your work has developed — managing your time, coping with pressure, etc. Some interviewers will ask these types of question, not necessarily in relation to your employment, but to give you the freedom to illustrate these qualities with the best examples you can give from all your life experiences. This is particularly useful for people who have not been in the employment market for very long and is essential for those entering it for the first time.

Q. How good are you at dealing with people?

A. It is something I really enjoy, I like contact with colleagues and clients and would generally describe myself as a sociable person. I am good at getting the level of my communication right; it doesn't matter whether it is someone who has come to fix the computer system or the finance director.

If you have encountered an exceptionally mean interviewer, you might get a response such as the following.

Q. So you spend a great deal of your time talking, does this leave you time to get on with the job you are supposed to be doing?

A. I know, I did make it sound rather like that didn't I? No, I take my responsibility for running the customer accounts section very seriously, but I have found that when you are chasing customers for money you often get more by being pleasant than by becoming the kind of person whose telephone calls they want to ignore.

Q. How good are your writing skills?

A. My main strength is that my writing skills are adaptable. Through my course I developed academic writing skills, but they are obviously not what is required in many business situations. I have been secretary for a local social club for a year or two which means I am good at taking notes and also writing basic business correspondence and I don't just rely on the spell checker on my computer, I'm quite happy to use a dictionary.

A. My business studies course at school meant we had to write business letters of various kinds and I always got good marks for those and for my English assignments. I am already the one in our family who ends up writing official letters if anyone needs to write them — actually it's something I really enjoy.

Q. What level and range of computer skills do you have?

A. I am quick and efficient with Word and Excel — I am more used to a PC, but I have spent a bit of time using Macs. I don't use IT in my present job, but I have a home computer and keeping up with helping my children with their homework really got me interested, so I did an evening course 18 months ago. I am quite comfortable with email and the internet.

Q. Give me an example of your negotiating skills.

A. I recently persuaded various local shops and small businesses to take out paid advertising space in a programme for a fund raising day in aid of our community sports centre. It was really hard at first. People weren't out and out unwilling, but they were often quite disinterested and had to be nudged several times before they would come up with any money. I got good at being pushy without upsetting people. We raised more than £3,000 in the end.

A. It sounds like a small thing, but I share a house with three other people at the moment and actually persuading people to do their share of the cleaning, tidying and maintenance has been a really uphill struggle, especially when people are really resistant, but I have developed a combination of being assertive, firm and appreciative as soon as anyone helps out and it seems to be working.

Q. Tell me something about your financial management skills.

A. I was always quite good at basic arithmetic and I find it easy to manage my own budget — though obviously I wish it were a larger one I had to manage. I was treasurer for our local church fate last year, and I maintained all the records in Excel as well as presenting the final figures to the committee.

Q. What are you like at speaking to a group of people, giving a presentation to a small or fairly large group?

A. I have been used to it ever since my student days, we had to present papers in seminars on a regular basis and in all my jobs so far I have had to give presentations to groups of clients. At first, I found the larger groups more difficult, but I find that as long as I plan what I am going to say carefully, make sure I have good visual aids and stick to an agreed time limit it goes well — I prefer smaller groups, but that is because there is a greater opportunity for audience participation, discussion, etc.

Q. Describe an occasion when you have had to be diplomatic.

A. It was actually a work situation and one member of staff was always complaining to the extent where she got on everybody's nerves, but she was also incredibly sensitive and she was good at her job. I was not her manager, so it was not a case of using authority. I did have to be as tactful as I could, but I began by asking her how she thought her actions might affect others and we took it from there.

Tip

Candidates attending interviews or preparing CVs often ask what they should do about mentioning skills and interests which may be linked to political parties or religious groups. They are aware that this might sometimes be inappropriate or too personal, but for many job applicants it is a way in which they have developed considerable expertise, gained in confidence and acquired new skills. All you can really do is use common sense — if you are involved in something pretty mainstream, it should not raise hackles or eyebrows; if it is something more fringe, you are probably wiser not to use it. Think about who your employer is too and work out whether you are likely to elicit antagonism or approbation.

Whether you are thinking about your skills and qualities in the context of work, education, or other aspects of your life take note of those which are likely to be most relevant to the job for which you are being interviewed. Listening skills, and the ability to be empathetic are important for a personal counsellor; having a cool nerve and a refined sense of judgement are essential if you are buying and selling substantial amounts of money.

Talking about yourself, whether it is your interests, your achievements or your personality ought to be an enjoyable experience. If you find yourself in social situations where people want to find out more about you, you take it as a compliment, so allow this pleasant reaction to permeate your interview conversations too. Describing yourself feels like hard work, but talking about anything you have done which you have really enjoyed, whether it relates to work, home or leisure can give you the chance to appear at your most vivacious, communicative and relaxed.

Final tips on selling your personality while keeping hold of your soul

1. Be honest with yourself but kind to yourself.

2. Discuss your strengths and weaknesses with friends and colleagues.

3. When considering interests be as inclusive as you can — interests are not just defined leisure activities, they may relate to your work, e.g., information technology, your home, entertaining or garden design, or your community involvement, e.g., member of the PTA.

4. Relate all your activities and skills to the job for which you are applying.

Chapter six

choice

change

and chance

your career decisions — what
will interviewers want to know
and why?

The place you occupy, or would like to occupy, in the whirling world of work could be as a result of scrupulous planning, early certainty and ambition unswervingly pursued, luck, coincidence or serendipity — perhaps a combination of all of these. There are many psychological theories explaining the process of career choice and career decisions, but we are, for the most part, unaware of these as we make the journey through school, college and various periods of employment to reach the point where we are at present. We know that we thought about various options, talked to people observed images of various jobs and professions through books, television and films. We experience contact with many jobs first hand, teachers, doctors, sales staff, plumbers, lawyers, volcanologists (well, not many

Tip

If you are entering the job market for the first time, say on completing school or university, if you are joining a profession after completing your academic or professional training, if you are choosing a training course or making a significant change of direction on your career path, then these are the occasions when you are certain to encounter questions that explain your choice, your reasons for it and your commitment to it.

of us). With all this information, we rarely analyze exactly how we took a career decision and why. Then, we realize that we could be asked about this at an interview and the analysis begins.

Your CV or application form will tell the interviewer and remind you of the factual part of your career history. You should turn your attention to the psychology that underpins it — your motivations, your decisions, your choices and your perceptions could all be up for scrutiny as part of your interview. As was mentioned in the introduction to this book, it is not possible to go through all the career and choices and infinite combinations of possible changes of direction, but the following questions and answers illustrate how this topic is likely to be raised at an interview and the answers outline some suitable responses. These questions and answers are easily adapted to match your own situation.

Q. **You say you know a job in advertising is right for you, why?**

A. When I was still at school one of my projects involved helping design programmes for a fund raising day for the school and I got very interested in the look of the programme and what would make people want to buy it. After that I managed to get a few day's work experience with an ad agency and that showed me how much more there is to it behind the scenes before an ad ever appears on TV or in a magazine, or on a poster. Most of my employment has been in sales, but always with a view to getting into advertising and capitalizing on the communication skills the sales jobs have developed. I am fascinated by what makes customers choose particular brands (customers, including me); what are the selling points that people really go for?

Tip

Questions asking why you want a particular job or course are frequently designed to ensure that a career choice you have made is more than a fantasy. A good TV drama with a forensic scientist or barrister as a charismatic main character has a significant, if temporary effect on career choice.

Q.   Why do you want to go to medical school?

A.   I suppose to begin with, it was something of a fantasy career, something I had always said I would do. Actually, all through school I have always been very strong on the sciences, but interested in people and social issues too and more and more medicine has begun to seem like a really suitable choice for me and one that I feel highly committed to. I have done some voluntary work at my local hospital and although that isn't medical experience, I feel quite comfortable in the hospital environment and enjoy talking to patients.

Q.   How do you think you would cope with the stress, the emotional side of the work, dealing with people who are very ill or dying, breaking bad news to them?

A.   I know that would be difficult and that I haven't yet been tested in those types of situation, but I know just from my own limited experience of being a patient with minor complaints how being listened to and having things explained carefully helps. I hope that during my training I would learn to cope better and better with painful situations, without losing an attitude of caring about patients and being interested in them as people. I would really like to be able to use the fact that I am strong on sciences in a socially worthwhile context.

Q.   You say you are interested in a career in investment management — explain your understanding of what investment management entails?

A.   My understanding is that I would be managing funds for corporate and private clients, researching performance of particular funds and reporting on those funds. I know that as well as my report writing and research skills I would have to be decisive, knowing when to buy, when to sell and when to just stay put for the time being. I like taking decisions, I do weigh up pros and cons, but I do it quickly, even if it is a simple thing like choosing a holiday destination or a new car.

Q. How did you reach your decision to become an occupational therapist?

A. For some time I had been considering a career in medicine and at school I was not aware of much beyond nursing or becoming a doctor, then through visiting a relative in hospital I came into contact with physiotherapy and occupational therapy and begun to look at the two carefully, talking to people in both professions. I like the amount of community work, home visits and a chance to support patients in so many aspects of their lives that occupational therapy provides. I love working with different people, it is a profession where I think I would be very happy and where I could give a lot.

Q. What skills do you think a teacher needs?

A. To enjoy working with young people and to have an infectious love of their own subject — I remember from my own time at school how easy it was to tell if a teacher really enjoyed what they were teaching and I certainly learned much better when they did. I don't think there is just one personality type who is successful, but you need to be a strong person, assertive and fair without being a bully. Respecting your students is important too. I have done a fair bit of community work with teenagers and I find my sense of humour goes a long way in building up good relationships.

Q. Have your career aspirations changed much over the years?

A. They have certainly developed and become more ambitious. When I was at school I had a vague idea that I wanted to do something connected with business, even though at the time that was a fairly nebulous concept to me. My business studies degree and my two years with my current company have refined my interests and I am strongly drawn to corporate finance. I am a good communicator, especially when it comes to handling negotiations — I worked with the mergers team for my current employer.

Tip

When you are asked a question which requires you to provide seemingly factual information, "what is involved in…" "what are essential skills for….." use the opportunity to blend in a positive comment about yourself, as is shown in many of the answers here.

Q. How do you stay well informed and up to date, on what is happening in your field?

A. I am an active member of my professional organization. As well as attending meetings and seminars I have run some training sessions myself. It's a real incentive to keep current if you are going to start imparting information to other people. I enjoy my profession, I see it as an interest as well as a career, so reading and discussing developments and issues is never a chore.

Q. Have you taken advantage of any staff development or training activities on offer over the past 12 months?

A. I have attended several conferences on long-term care to keep myself up to date with issues in the sector and I have also been on a team-building course, and two customer care courses. I try to take advantage of courses and conferences when they are on offer; you learn so much from networking as well as from the events themselves.

Q. How would you recommend your profession to someone who is considering joining?

A. I still find lecturing extremely satisfying, always dealing with new groups of students, human nature coming up with an infinite variety and I like my subject. I would have to warn anyone considering entering it now that it is very competitive and hard to get a permanent contract so they would have to be resilient as well as enthusiastic.

Q. How do you think your profession has changed since you first joined?

A. The impact of technology has to be the most significant thing. It has made some tasks such much easier and given me skills I never expected to acquire. It has also meant doing a great deal more of my own administration. In the end though, building up good relationships with clients is what counts and I believe that will always be a fundamental part of this work.

Describing your reasons for being in your current profession or your desire to make a change. In either of these circumstances, the following questionnaire will help you organize your thoughts.

Significant influences on your career decisions

Describe any influences that helped you reach your career decisions.

Family influences, e.g., jobs you became aware of through family members

Education influences, e.g., ideas triggered by courses or subjects you studied or projects you undertook

Significant influences on your career decisions

Influences through work experience, e.g., part-time jobs, holiday jobs, periods of employment before the one you are currently in

Influences through leisure interests, e.g., artistic/creative/cultural interests or new skills such as information technology, foreign languages

Influences through voluntary work or community activity

Changes influenced by your own changing perceptions and your personal development

Significant influences on your career decisions

Influences through planned information research about particular jobs, industries, professions, courses, etc.

If you are making a move within your current profession, you may find it useful to write a job description or a person specification as if you were doing the recruiting. You know which qualities in your own colleagues you find useful, desirable irritating or unacceptable — so try thinking from the interviewer's point of view.

Changing horses in mid race

Changing direction on your career path means you have already asked yourself some searching questions about why you want to make such a move. It may mean that you have had to take a step down the career ladder to make a move, or perhaps that you have given up employment for a while to return to education or further training of some kind. The searching questions that you will have asked yourself and the decision process that you went through to bring about a change of course will be subject matter for any interviewer as you work your way into your newly chosen career. When you are called for interview, your new employer will want to reassure him or herself, that not only do you have appropriate skills, experience and personal qualities to fit in and do the job, but that you are sure about the direction in which you are now heading. You will face all the usual questions about education, interests, work experience, strengths and weaknesses, but in addition you will need to have some good answers for questions specifically exploring your change of direction.

Remember that you would not have been asked to the interview if you weren't already seen as a potential successful employee — don't fall into the trap of feeling criticized because you have altered your original career path — this could mean that you have even more to offer than the more typical candidate.

Q. **Tell me why you chose to go to university after you had been working in retailing for 15 years.**

A. Most of all, because I wanted to. At the back of my mind I had always regretted not staying on at school and continuing with my education, I had been quite successful in my retail career, I started as a junior assistant and I was manager of a large branch before I went back into education. I also believed it would help me make the break into other business and move away from the retail trade.

Q. **How difficult did you find it returning to education as a mature student?**

A. It was hard at first and I certainly missed the regular salary. I had the idea that most of the course would be full of young students who had just left school, but as it turned out there was a very broad mix on my course. I found a lot of my work and life experience was relevant to issues that we discussed on the course and I was often able to give real examples of situations, rather than relying on textbook answers.

Q. **Before you did your degree, you were working as a nurse and now you are applying for work in management consultancy — how do you explain such a change of direction?**

A. I don't regret the seven years I spent in nursing, but I believe I made a career decision before I was ready to and as the result of considerable family pressure. My years in nursing have not been wasted. I developed excellent interpersonal skills, coped with stress and worked well under pressure, I also acquired good administrative skills and experience in training and managing other staff. There are so many problems to be solved when you are dealing with people and their health, and I am sure seeing your way to the heart of a problem is something that will be immensely useful to me in management consultancy. I think my calm attitude and common sense approach would go down well with clients.

Q. Journalism is extremely competitive — your background in engineering is, to say the least, unusual, so what makes you think you could succeed in this profession?

A. Before I trained as an engineer I had considered technical journalism as an option. I always did well in English as well as the technical subjects at school, but I was very drawn to designing and producing something tangible rather than talking about it. As I have progressed at work I have looked for more at the trade press and often thought I could write a more readable article than some of the material I have come across. I have had articles published in a motor cycle magazine and several of my letters have appeared in the local press and occasionally the national press. My CV outlines my IT skills and I know how important they are in journalism today.

Nightmare to avoid

By all means be as creative as you can in making links from past career to present choice, but it can be stretched too far. One candidate being interviewed to join the Royal Air Force said he was applying because he wanted to be an astronaut and the Air Force was the next best thing. Asked what his relevant experience was to date, he said he had been working on the bacon counter in his local supermarket.

Q. How do we know this change of career direction won't just be a passing phase, you might have another change of heart after we have invested time and money in your training and progress.

A. Well I believe the fact that I have put so much commitment into making the change is a clear demonstration. Studying for my law exams on a part-time basis was very demanding and I had to be really single minded about it. My work in housing management meant that I often dealt with people who had legal issues to deal with and I gained some familiarity with the court system through the cases we actually took to court. It is not always easy to make a career decision at 18 that will see you through the rest of your life, but I am quite convinced that the law will hold my interest for at least a couple of decades.

A. I have used IT a great deal in my current and previous job and although my job description might say 'administrator', I am always the one in the office who troubleshoots if we have problems with the computer side of things and if I can't solve it I liase with our technical department — I usually end up training new staff on our systems too. I think I have already made the career change by stealth, but obviously I would like a job where I could develop these skills to a higher level. My interpersonal skills are good and I think this is a skill that is sometimes neglected by staff working mainly with machines and electronic systems.

Q. Would you honestly have considered work in this field if you hadn't been made redundant?

A. It is true that sales is a new direction for me, but I am very keen and I certainly get on well with people. Being a good supervisor means getting people to do what you want without bullying them and I guess in some ways sales might be similar to that — you want a customer to buy your office supplies, but you want them to feel it's a good decision that they have taken themselves. Having a practical and technical background also means I would be confident demonstrating anything I was selling. I am not saying I was pleased to be made redundant, but a move like this could be good for me and, of course, for my new employer.

Q. It sounds as if you are somewhat disillusioned with your career in social work/electronics/health and safety, is there an element of you running away from it rather than actually making a positive choice now?

A. Perhaps a part of me is trying to escape, but that doesn't mean I am not making a carefully reasoned and, I think, wise decision about what I should do next. The skills I have acquired and the qualities I have developed have changed me enormously over the past ten years and I know there are parts of me that are not being utilized half as effectively as they could be.

(At this point it is important to give a concrete example of an aspect of yourself that you feel your newly chosen career would utilize, but also emphasize the strengths you already have.)

Q. How do you feel about having to start at the bottom again, becoming a trainee, when you have had considerable responsibility in your last job?

A. I don't mind at all, I have always been interested in book publishing, in anything to do with books really and the years I spent in teaching have given me a discerning eye when it comes to spotting a good educational book. I am sure I shall enjoy my training and learn quickly and I see it as a really exciting opportunity.

Q. Because of your lack of experience in this field, we couldn't pay you what you are being paid in your current accountancy job. How will you cope with taking a drop in salary?

A. Well at least my accounting experience means I am good at making the best of any budget and of course I looked very carefully at the financial implications of my decision. I hope my contribution to the company will mean my salary is reviewed in the not too distant future, but I can definitely accept the job on what you are currently able to offer.

Q. **How do you deal with change in general?**

A. I am quite used to it. There were many changes caused by external factors in my previous job and I think it is really a case of learning not to see it as a threat, but as a chance to look at new ways of doing things. When my last department was amalgamated with another section there were all kinds of anxieties about how we would lose specialist knowledge and expertise, but we ended up all becoming more well informed and more able to help clients effectively.

> **Tip**
>
> Don't be daunted by these hostile sounding questions. They are there to address real concerns that the interviewer has and once again, to test your commitment.

It is important to be candid and open about your decision, without feeling obliged to give away private information that is none of your employer's business. You don't have to pretend that you have always had a secret desire to be a train driver, tight-rope walker or whatever else you are moving into. You do have to be clear on what your reasons are and very convincing about your staying power and commitment.

In some ways, all this emphasis on explaining career choice and career decisions is surprising. We inhabit a world where the nature of employment has changed and is still changing in this new century. We are frequently told not to expect the notion of a continuous and smoothly progressing career. Economic circumstances, technological change and global markets all contribute to the need to be highly adaptable and flexible in your approach to work — indeed these are exactly the skills most interviewers claim to be seeking. It is one of the many burdens of being an interviewee that you are arguing a case for your capacity to cope with change when a few minutes earlier you have been persuading the interviewer that you are a creature capable of planning, organizing and anticipating.

Final tips on career choice and career change

1. Review your past to analyze where you are now.

2. Consider the key skills you need to do your current job.

3. Think about the major satisfactions and frustrations associated with that job.

4. Ask yourself how you would sell your chosen career to somebody else.

5. If you are planning a change of direction, list the main reasons why.

Chapter seven

onwards and upwards

Why are you the right person for this job, your next job and wherever else you want to be?

What role do ambition, drive, career progress and career success play in your life and how would you even begin to define some of those terms as they fit your circumstances? The reason prospective employers are so interested in these aspects of you is that they link to something very important to all employers — your level of motivation; that all important question "will you do the job?" Assuming you have the qualifications, the right experience, an attractive CV and a pleasant interview manner, your interviewer needs to be able to recognize real commitment. Do you really, really want the job — not the job offer and the chance to turn up three weeks on Monday — but the chance to do the work, meet the customers, fit in with the team, contribute to profits, status and quality, to the organization's future.

What motivates each of us is different, material reward, public acclaim, artistic achievement, contributing to society, breaking new ground, or simply finding work a reasonably pleasant place to be where we can go home at the end of the day with a clear conscience and enjoy a good bottle of wine and an untroubled sleep.

Look at the work values mentioned here and think about which of them is most important to you. You may wish to add others that are not featured on this list.

I am able to get ahead in my chosen career.

I can help people cope better with their lives — their circumstances.

The financial rewards are significant.

There is at least some degree of job security.

I have the opportunity to work on my own.

My work involves some risks, not necessarily physical, could be financial or in terms of taking potentially risky decisions.

There may be opportunities to travel.

The social status attached to the job is very high.

There is an opportunity to be creative or inventive.

The work is socially useful.

There is a lot of autonomy in the work situation.

There are opportunities to work as part of a team.

There are opportunities to work with other people, customers, clients or other professionals.

There is a busy, high pressure atmosphere.

There is not too much stress involved.

There are opportunities to use specific skills, such as information technology, foreign languages, design skills, for example.

There are plenty of opportunities to train and motivate others.

There is considerable responsibility at an early stage in my career.

There are opportunities for further professional training.

There are opportunities to use interpersonal skills, persuading, negotiating, etc.

My ideas can make a real contribution to the way work is carried out.

There is considerable variety in the daily/weekly/monthly tasks I undertake.

Opportunity to use good writing skills.

Opportunity to use mathematical skills.

Situation where pay is related to performance.

There are plenty of opportunities for promotion.

It is likely that you are driven by a combination of many of the different factors above and that you are already involved in, or looking for work that at least attempts to match this profile. If you are clear about what motivates you, it will help you to answer some of the questions that interviewers confront you with to check out your motivation and enthusiasm.

 How did you get your first job?

A. I made applications to all the travel agents that I could reasonably get to without moving home and the third one that interviewed me offered me a job. I can still remember it so clearly — I knew it was a competitive area to get into and I was really thrilled at getting the chance to do something that interested me.

A. I went to talk to someone who was a friend of a friend who was fairly senior in this local small manufacturing company and I was offered a job. I wasn't even sure if I wanted it at that stage, but I was certainly glad of the offer.

A. I qualified just as we went into a recession, so I had to make a lot of applications, send off dozens of CVs, make what felt like hundreds of telephone calls, though it probably wasn't that many. Eventually I got into a local law firm by offering to do some voluntary work, just photocopying, taking over on reception, that sort of thing, but they ended up taking me on and putting me through the rest of my qualifications.

Q. **How did you get your current job?**

A. I was approached by a recruitment consultant who was looking for someone to head up a new division being created by my current employer. I faced quite a difficult decision, because I had enjoyed my previous job and the company had treated me well, but in the end, this was a new challenge, and a financially rewarding one, so I took the decision to make the move. I have been there for three and a half years now and the division is running smoothly, so I feel ready to move on.

A. As I was making something of a change of direction, from engineering production management to technical authorship, I started applying to any suitable adverts in the national and specialist press as well as approaching some places on spec. In the end, I got my current post through an advert in the trade press.

> **Tip**
>
> Make it clear that whether you had a stroke of good luck, or faced considerable difficulty when looking for work, you remained active, in control and prepared to take decisions.

Q. Why have you decided to leave your current job?

A. I am still enjoying my work and my last appraisal suggested I am ready to take on more management responsibility, but it seems unlikely that the business will grow for the next year or two — I don't want to get into the position where I am just coasting.

Q. What could you do to make your job more interesting then, if you are saying it isn't really challenging you?

(In other words, whose fault is it you are coasting, is it you or your employer?)

A. I have already taken some measures — I have volunteered to take on more responsibility for staff training and I recently initiated a new customer satisfaction survey — but I still feel I could be doing more, especially in managing and motivating larger sales teams.

Other possible reasons for leaving a job include the following.

A. I had anticipated and been told that a major part of my current job would involve designing, developing and maintaining the organization's website, this was what really grabbed me about the job and also what my qualifications and my previous job had prepared me for. I was quite happy to help out with other administrative tasks within the department, I accept that you all need to help out, but actually administration has ended up taking up about 70 per cent of my time, the website seems to be a low priority and I don't want to lose my skills through lack of use.

A. I hadn't been planning to leave, it is only when I saw this position advertised that I really felt it was an opportunity not to be missed. I really welcome the idea of being able to use my writing skills as well as my IT skills — they are my major work interests, so I just had to give this one a go.

Whether you are seeking promotion, or a job on a similar level to the one you hold at present, interviewers want to know if you are difficult to work with.

Q. How do you react if a colleague criticizes your work?

A. It depends how valid I believe the criticism to be and to some extent how it is put to me, but I do listen to the point being made and try not to be too sensitive. I like to be able to share ideas and suggestions with other people and sometimes what seems like an adverse comment has taught me something very useful.

Q. How do you react if you don't get your way over a work issue?

A. It would depend on how crucial I think that issue is to our business. One of our senior managers wanted to bring in changes that would have altered everyone's jobs and responsibilities and I felt that this would actually mean a far less effective service to our clients with a lot of specialist knowledge being lost. I was very against the idea, but I put my arguments down very thoroughly and I hoped quite persuasively on paper, so that management would have ample opportunity to consider my point of view. To my delight it worked and the plans were shelved. Of course, it does not always work in my favour like that, but I know I can make a persuasive argument when I have to and I can also accept the decisions of others if necessary.

Q.   What do you think of your current manager?

A.   She is very effective, especially at delegating the right tasks to the right people and I have learned a lot from her. If I were to make a criticism it is that I think she could achieve more by involving wider groups of staff in consultation before decisions are made — sometimes she loses goodwill from an otherwise highly motivated staff team.

Q.   What do you think of your current employer?

A.   As an employer, they are fine and I have no complaints, but I would like to see them being a little more imaginative about the range of fashion clothes we retail. Working on the buying side, it can be frustrating when you feel you have good ideas and there is not really an outlet for them, of course you have to accept that not all your ideas will be good ones, but our sales figures were not brilliant for last year, as you know, so we do need to do something.

Q.   How do you maintain your interest in your current job?

A.   Quite easily. I am working on several accounts each for different clients and so my work has a lot of variety, both on a daily and on a more long-term basis. No two accounts are ever the same even if, in theory, the process that you go through is almost identical.

Nightmare to avoid

Saying that your current boss is the most hideous and evil megalomaniac that ever walked the planet and that you have serious doubts as to whether he is even from this planet and then finding he is a close personal friend of the chair of the interview panel. Careful, measured criticism of your current role/organization may be okay, but whining and whinging is definitely out. Loyalty is a quality that is highly prized by all employers, so even if you are currently working for a competitor, appearing disloyal will not gain you friends.

Tip

Be ready for questions about what you earn and what you expect to earn, especially if you are entering work where there is not a pre-set salary structure. If you are unsure what you should be paid, have a look at what similar jobs with similar organizations are paying before you commit yourself.

Q. What is your current salary?

A. I am currently paid ....., though if I remain with my current employer I am expecting an increase in three months' time. Pay rises are linked to annual appraisals and I have received an increase every year so far.

A. I currently receive ...., but I would hope to better that if I were to be offered a post here.

Q. What salary are you expecting us to pay you?

A. My current salary is ..... and I do expect to better that when I take up a new post. Looking at your job description I see the job with you as being more demanding and that is one of the reasons I have applied, but I would hope that increased responsibility would be reflected in what you are prepared to pay me.

A. Moving from an organization with a fixed salary structure it is a new experience for me to be negotiating my own pay, but I have researched what a current reasonable rate for this job would be and I know I am well qualified and keen, so I would expect at least ..... .

Q. Do you think you are being paid enough?

A. I know that what I am paid equates favourably to others on a similar level in my profession — but I am prepared to put in extra time and extra effort and I believe it is reasonable that I should be rewarded for this.

A. Not really, I took on the position at a fairly low salary because at that stage I did not have much direct experience in the field, but I caught up quickly and I have a good track record. I intend to negotiate for more money if I remain in my current situation and I expect a degree of success in my negotiations.

Tip

Unless you are very unusual, you probably don't enjoy discussing what salary you expect to be paid and yet on many occasions it is a significant factor in what has prompted you to apply for a new job. Two important points. Don't sell yourself cheap, the interviewer can always negotiate down, so in general ask for a bit more than you think is acceptable. Work out what your bottom line really is. The second point, you won't be rejected just because you asked for too much money, the worst that can happen is that the company will say "sorry, no can do".

Q. Where do you see yourself in three years' time?

A. As I have only just entered the physiotherapy profession, part of me would like to keep my options open, learn as much as I can and gain from the different specialisms I shall come into contact with over the coming years. I really enjoyed my work on neurology during my training, so that may be a direction I choose. Management does interest me in the longer term, but I want several years of working with patients before I move in that direction.

A. This is a lively and expanding company by all accounts and from what I have learned so far, so I very much hope that I shall still be here in three years' time. I chose to apply for your customer operations division because it seems to me a great way to learn a lot about your services, your customers and your finances. I do, however, have an open mind about moving into other divisions, if this helped me learn more and prepared me more effectively for senior management.

Self promotion

Promotion interviews can be demanding since you are not only illustrating how well you work in your current role or profession, but also being asked to demonstrate that you are suitable to take on more, to face new challenges accept new tasks and so to some extent — whatever evidence you produce — you are partly being taken on trust.

It makes no difference whether this promotion is within your current organization or whether you are taking the opportunity to change employers at the same time as you take a step up the ladder. On both occasions you will have to convince your interviewer of your suitability.

Q. What do you want out of this promotion?

A. Of course, I want the opportunity to take on more responsibility, but specifically, I know that a job at this level will mean more opportunity to contribute to decisions. I like the fact that the job would require me to get involved in strategic planning. My past project planning experience will prove very useful in this respect.

A. I know this job will involve less direct contact with customers, but I think I can serve our customers better by taking responsibility for training other staff in customer care and for developing policies that enhance customer support. I have enjoyed my customer contact and used it to learn about what they see as good service and what really irritates them — I would love the chance to act on this. I can give you some ideas if you like.

Nightmare to avoid

At one particular promotion interview, each candidate had been asked to pre-pare a brief presentation to put to the panel. Materials were provided for this purpose. One candidate boldly announced that he was not going to use loads of fancy coloured pens and time-wasting charts like the nitwit who preceded him (he had seen what he thought was a previous candidate's handiwork in the preparation room — it turned out to be a chart prepared with time and effort by none other than one of the interview panel for a training meeting session the following day). Not a winning strategy.

Q.   **What new ideas would you bring to the job that other candidates would not?**

A.   I would spend some time getting to know the department, so that I could assess what was already working well, but also see whether there were areas where we could be more efficient. My recent management diploma gave me the opportunity to look closely at how to get the best skills mix in work groups, getting better results for the company and higher job satisfac-tion among staff members. I see that you do have project groups within the department, so some of my ideas could be very effective here.

A.   I became good at finding creative solutions to problems both logistical and practical when I did two years of voluntary serv-ice overseas. Quite often it was impossible to get either the equipment or the personnel that you would ideally have liked, so you just had to work with whatever was available. I was involved in building projects, so obviously we could not com-promize safety, but I certainly learned to be flexible.

Q.   How tough are you if it comes to disciplining a staff member?

(This question is not exclusive to promotion, but such responsibilities tend to increase as you climb the professional ladder.)

A.   It is a situation I have already had to deal with in my current job where I had a staff member with a very poor time-keeping record. We tried to be flexible because of his domestic situation, but being flexible is very different to allowing someone to take advantage. I would be as firm as was necessary, double-check the rules and regulations and legal situation before I jumped in, but I would also be sure I was being fair. Where necessary I would consult with other appropriate staff.

Q.   You haven't been in your current post very long, do you think you are ready for this promotion?

A.   Of course, I feel confident and very excited about the prospect of becoming a deputy head. I may not have been in teaching for that many years, but I came into the profession as a mature person, with considerable work experience behind me and having my own children in school before I started teaching has given me a well-grounded understanding of the issues that face the profession, the changing demands and pressures that we face. I believe I am the kind of leader that draws colleagues with me, rather than one who pushes them from behind.

Q.   You are probably aware that other colleagues in your section have applied for this promotion. How will you cope if there is any resentment if we offer you the job?

A.   It is common knowledge that three of us have applied and we all know there is only one job, so I think any of us would be mature about it. I think the best way to avoid resentment is to involve colleagues in appropriate consultation; if they have good ideas, use them. If slight resentment turned into a real attitude problem, obviously I would tackle them directly about this and hope that having it out would clear the air.

Q. How will you feel if you don't get this promotion?

A. Naturally it will be a disappointment, it is something I really want, I feel ready for it and I think I have had plenty of experience in all aspects of the hotel business and this particular hotel. However, I still enjoy my current job as deputy manager so I don't imagine I would immediately become disillusioned and lose interest in my work.

Q. This position would make considerable demands on your qualities as a leader. What would you say is your leadership style?

A. I am a strong leader and I suppose I would describe myself as a bit of a shaper, good with new ideas and quick to spot how to delegate effectively and take on appropriate work myself. I have learned a lot about my management style from working on joint projects with managers of other departments where I have had to work in a more co-operative way. This has been useful, I am still a strong leader, but I have learned the value of consultation and of making the best use of the skills every team member has.

Tip

An awkward question can arise if you are applying for a job which is viewed by your interviewer as being on the same level as the job you currently have, so be ready for it.

Q. This job looks quite similar to the one you are currently doing, why have you applied for it?

A. It is true that your job description looks quite similar to the one I am working to at present, but I really don't believe any two jobs are exactly the same, different customers, different projects and different approaches. I am ambitious, but I believe one of the ways to realize that ambition is to gain a thorough understand of the business first. I see this move as a very exciting one.

Q. Do you think you are overqualified for this job?

A. No I don't. I think my experience and qualifications will mean that I can do the job very effectively from day one and be a very useful member of the department straight away. I have been keen to work in a smaller company like this ever since I left university, I would enjoy the job and you would get a good new member of staff.

Tip

Be prepared for questions where, as they say in the money markets "it's time to sell, sell, sell" and the product is you. This applies whether you are seeking promotion, or reflects a change or a move.

Q. We are seeing several candidates today, what makes you stand out from the others?

A. All my qualifications and experience relates directly to what your job description says you require, but more than that, your plan to expand into Europe ties in very well with my recent spell in Paris. The staff I have met here today and this interview has convinced me that I would fit in extremely well here and would really enjoy it, which is always a great motivator.

Q. Give me the three main reasons why we should give you this job?

A. As I already manage a health centre with real success I can certainly demonstrate that I can do the job. In addition, I am good at coming up with and acting on new ideas. For example I developed a scheme where more of our patients could access different complementary therapies and yet this had minimal financial impact on our overall budget. Team skills are one of my real strengths. It is so easy when several different groups of professionals are involved for work situations to become divisive or competitive in an unhelpful way. I am good at fostering understanding and co-operation between different work groups. On top of those reasons, I am really enthusiastic about this post, I would put a great deal of energy into it.

Q. Would you take this job if we offered it to you?

A. Yes, definitely, I was keen as soon as I saw your advert and your job description fits my skills and experience very well. More than that, actually meeting potential colleagues and finding out more about your current activities has clarified still further what an exciting challenge it would be to work here.

> **Tip**
>
> Be careful with this last one; many interviewers ask this as a standard question to all candidates, so it does not mean they have decided to offer you the job. Nevertheless, be positive and enthusiastic and only if you have real reservations that mean you are pretty half-hearted anyway, should you express any of these.

Seeking promotion, or seeking a change — in both cases you must recognize new or different aspects of the work as well as those that are similar to your current or previous positions, so that you are not caught out with comments such as "well you haven't done anything quite like this before".

Final tips on showing that you've got what it takes

1. Consider what really is important to you about your work.

2. Prepare for questions that focus on your loyalty and your commitment.

3. Link past experience to any new responsibilities and tasks that you are aware will form part of the job that you are applying for.

Chapter eight

your
Achilles' heel

Dealing with your weak spots,
difficult questions, embarrassing
pauses and horrible interviews

Unless you are one of those rare people who have led a charmed life and found that every decision has turned out well and that fortune has always smiled on you, you are likely to have aspects of your past (be it poor examination results, a period of unemployment, a patchy work history, poor health record, etc.) that you don't want to be asked about at job interviews. Yet you know that, because these issues are part of your history, they are likely to emerge from your CV, application form or employment and character references, that they are very likely to arouse a future employer's curiosity. Interviewers do want an explanation of results or circumstances that appear to contradict other evidence of your history and character, and leaves them wondering "Why?"

Before preparing your answers on any tricky questions that may be applicable to you, you must remind yourself that interviewers ask these things because they genuinely want to know — they want to ascertain whether some weak spot was a temporary glitch or reflects a more pervasive problem. The good news is that they suspect it is the former — otherwise they would not have invited you to the interview in the first place. There can be a second reason why you may be questioned on these 'Achilles' heels' — interviewers know that you are likely to feel vulnerable on these and they want to see whether you become hostile or defensive, or whether you take the opportunity to use your skills of communication, persuasion, analysis and calm reason to offer plausible and convincing explanations.

A brief word about truth

This book does not promise to offer a rigorous analysis of the philosophical and moral place of truth in the competitive jungle of job hunting. It does, however offer some common sense advice on this subject. If you are hiding something on your CV and/or during a job interview, you are unlikely to communicate so effectively or be as relaxed and natural as you would like to be. Things which you have chosen not to say, fictional exam results, jobs that you invent or references written by your Mum to enhance your case may well trip you up. Employers almost always take up references before they employ you and if you have to hide the truth at an interview then you have to ask yourself how you are going to keep this up if you are the successful candidate. Remember also, that if an employer finds out later that you have not been straight with them, they may use this as grounds for dismissal or other disciplinary procedures.

Here are some of the issues about which candidates feel anxious — and some suggested ways to deal with these.

Q. I see that you got very good GCSE results and yet your A level results are poor — what happened?

A. I was unsure of whether I wanted to stay on at school and do A levels, it was something my parents pushed for, but my heart was not really in it. I had become too interested in other things and I just didn't put in the effort I should.

A possible follow-up question to this that could easily provoke a defensive response might be as follows.

Q. Can I take it then, that if you don't like something, you stop working hard at it. What if we give you a job and you find there are parts of it you don't enjoy?

A. I have had a good work record for the past three years, since I left school and I have had no difficulty in handing several fairly routine, repetitive tasks during that time. I have grown up a lot since I was 17, I seem to learn better in a work, rather than a school environment. I am doing an evening course in website design though, and I am really enjoying that.

Q. There appears to be an eight-month gap on your CV? What were you doing during this time?

A. I had been temping for the previous two years and I really wanted something with more of a sense of direction. With hindsight, I might have done better to wait until I had something permanent before I gave up the temporary work, but I really wanted to concentrate on my job search and give it 100 per cent. I wasn't expecting the job market to plummet so badly during that time. I got my act together by doing a short, intensive course in secretarial skills and was very pleased to get back into the work environment.

Q. You only got a third class degree. We are really looking for someone with a good honours degree.

(Remember, whatever they say, they have still chosen to interview you.)

A. Of course, I was disappointed I had hoped for an upper second and my first two years' results indicated that I would achieve this. I had a lot of personal problems during my final year which are well behind me and sorted out now, but they did affect my result. My individual and group project results were good and I think these developed the communication, time management and information gathering skills that I need for this particular post — so I know I am strong on useful, relevant work skills.

Q. From your CV, it looks as if you have taken six years out of the job market — how do you think you will fit in coping with the routine and the demands of work?

(Candidates should not have to see this as a negative area in their past, but sometimes it can feel that way.)

A. Yes I took a break from paid work to have my children and see them settled into school, I have not had salaried employment for the past few years, but I have actually been working very hard. Bringing up a family makes you deal with the unexpected as well as the routine and I often work a much longer day than I did when I was in paid employment. Besides, I certainly haven't forgotten all the skills I used in the drawing office. I keep up to date with the relevant trade press and more significantly by doing some drawing work for friends.

Tip

This one applies to answers on any topic, not just awkward ones. Avoid using apologetic sounding words or phrases such as 'only', a 'little' 'limited' or 'not much' when you describe any of your experience, look for alternatives like, 'useful', 'considerable', 'extensive' and 'relevant'.

Q. I see that you were made redundant by your last employer nine months ago — how have you coped with this?

A. It was not a complete surprise because the company had been in financial difficulties for a while and many of us were aware that our jobs might be under threat, nevertheless it was a shock and very hard at first. I've always been someone with an optimistic attitude, but this field is competitive at the moment. I enrolled on an IT course to give me some new design skills very soon after I lost my last job and I have also been doing some voluntary work for my local secondary school, helping with computer skills classes. My CAD skills have certainly developed significantly since leaving my last company and I am very eager to get back into full-time work.

Q. You don't think you will have lost a bit of your edge and slipped out of the work routine during that time?

(This is one possible, rather mean reply).

A. Quite the opposite. I have filled my time constructively and increased my skills, but I really enjoyed work. I think my energy levels and enthusiasm are on top form and I intend them to stay that way.

Q. It looks from your CV as if you haven't had much work experience at all — other candidates we are seeing today are likely to have had far more.

A. I did think about working for a year before I went to university and I had intended to take on a part-time job while I was studying. In fact, my father was very ill for a major part of my course and I ended up helping out a lot at home and spending time with him and my family. My course was quite practical and as you can see I got a good result even with all the stress going on outside. I really believe I am capable of doing this job and doing it well and you do emphasize your high standard of training and induction.

A. It was really difficult to find the sort of work I wanted when I first left school. I was desperate to get into something with the media and it was hard for me to accept that that just may not be possible at that time. I did do some voluntary work for my local hospital radio and some unpaid work experience with two local newspapers — I guess I should have mentioned those on my CV.

Tip

It is all too common for job applicants to dismiss part of their own useful experience as irrelevant. Voluntary work, work shadowing, work experience and helping out with a family business are frequent examples of this neglect.

Q. Why did you drop out of university before you had completed your course?

A. It was the wrong subject and the wrong time and place for me. I had been reluctant to carry on with my studies and I am afraid my first year results showed that. The evening job I was doing at the local sports centre was far more exciting to me and the manager was very happy with me. If I go back to studying I want it to be on a part-time basis and I want it to be a more practical course than the degree I started.

It is difficult when, as a candidate, you know that there are extremely private and personal reasons which have affected an area of your life at a particular time — it may have been a bereavement, serious illness of someone close to you, a broken relationship or marriage, or problems within your family at an important time during your schooling. You are reluctant to reveal information which feels personal and private, which might make you feel upset and your interviewer embarrassed and which quite frankly it beyond the scope of what a prospective employer has a reasonable right to know.

Balanced against this, is your knowledge that the facts of your personal circumstances at the time offer a legitimate and understandable explanation for a drop in your work or academic performance. It is perfectly reasonable to say that you were affected by difficult personal circumstances that you would rather not discuss at an interview but, if it is something you feel comfortable about mentioning then do so. A family break up during your school examinations or a marriage falling apart just as you applied for a promotion may be something you would rather reveal and get it out of the way. Even the least well trained of interviewers should not then follow this up with a run of personal and intrusive questions. It is also helpful to add a comment suggesting that whatever a problem was it is now behind you and is not affecting your performance any longer. That, after all, is what the person who is contemplating paying your salary and investing in your training and development really wants to know.

Q. You have changed jobs rather frequently in the last few years, does this mean you get restless if you are in any job for a considerable length of time?

A. Some of my recent moves have been because I have needed to relocate to different places for personal reasons. I am now settled here and have recently bought a property in the area. Of all the jobs I have done in the past three years I really enjoyed my work at the finance company. I have very good references from them and the work I was doing looks very similar to the responsibilities you list in your advert and job spec.

A. Many of those jobs were temporary anyway and my employers in those situations were not expecting me to stay long, for example when I was providing Christmas or holiday cover. I did not want to commit myself to a career until I was more sure of the direction in which I wanted to go. My temporary job in the local planning department gave me my first real involvement with work that touched on environmental issues and I have done a great deal of voluntary work with urban and rural environmental improvement projects, so I hope that demonstrates my enthusiasm and commitment to a career with your organization — it feels like the opportunity I have been waiting for.

Q. You have requested us not to approach your current employer for a reference. Why aren't you happy for us to do this?

A. My current company may be looking at some cost-cutting measures and if they think I am looking elsewhere I may turn out to be one of them. I am quite happy with my work there, but I have been at that level for two and a half years now and I think the job you are offering is ideal. I feel sure I would enjoy it, but I can't guarantee that I shall be the successful candidate and I don't want to unsettle things with my current firm.

A. My current manager has only been in post for three months and if he were asked to write my reference I am not sure that he knows enough about my work, what it entails, what my strengths are, or to be able to do justice to my skills. I feel you would get far more relevant information from my previous boss, for whom I worked for four and a half years.

Q. Your reference shows that last year you had 15 days off work due to sickness. Is this a typical annual record for you?

A. No, far from it. Those 15 days were all in a block and it was because I had had an accident while on a skiing holiday. My attendance record up to then has been pretty good.

Q. Apart from your annual leave entitlement and public holidays, how many days were you absent from work last year?

A. Four — two were for dental surgery and the other two for an extremely heavy cold that meant I was useless on the telephone, but I am usually pretty hardy.

Health records are of concern to employers. Many organizations will use a pro forma reference request which they send to your current employer or your nominated referee. This form usually contains a section asking for details of how many days you have taken off work due to sickness, so your interviewer may already have access to accurate, factual information on this.

Q. What is your time keeping like?

A. Good, I am usually the first to arrive in the mornings and I dislike being late for any meeting, training session or anything. I think you owe it to your colleagues as well as your manager to be punctual.

Q. You left your last job without having another one lined up to go to, wasn't that a bit risky?

A. Yes, I suppose it was, but I had never intended to stay in sales for that long and it felt like the right decision. There had been a lot of changes there recently and very few staff were happy. It takes a great deal for me to become discouraged. But I felt my wisest option was to leave and start looking for something else.

The sales work was useful, especially dealing with people and working under pressure — two things which I have become very good at — I'm sure they would be valuable in your customer support department.

Q. One of your references suggests that you sometimes lose your cool in the office. What is your reaction to this?

A. It has happened very occasionally, but I have always been quick to apologize if I have been unreasonable and it has certainly never happened in front of a client. I am aware of it, so I make an effort to keep calm and explain what is annoying or frustrating me. I think most of my colleagues would say that although I can be a little volatile, I am a helpful and supportive member of the department for the vast majority of the time.

Q. Have you ever been asked to resign?

A. No, but I have come close enough to it to resign of my own accord rather than waiting to be asked. We had undergone a restructuring with a new manager, with whom I admit I did not hit it off and yet I had worked successfully and productively there for ten years. I knew that cost cutting and streamlining measures were on the cards and I just had to accept that I was not flavour of the month. It was hard, but it was a useful lesson and I spent an interesting 18 months working as an independent consultant.

A. No, I am pleased to say, that is not an experience I have had to go through.

A. Yes. It was the first job I had after I left school. I really wanted to get into anything to do with cars and somehow I ended up working for an insurance company — I don't think it was ever going to work out.

Tip

Don't shoot yourself in the foot. If you have had awful experiences, losing jobs through no fault of your own, or even as a result of your own actions – if this is in the past, and won't emerge through references, don't mention it.

What am I supposed to say?

Some interviewers will try to find out more about your strengths and weaknesses by confronting you with imaginary scenarios to see just how good you are at thinking on your feet. These questions are not designed with one 'right' answer, so don't waste time agonizing over exactly what you think the correct solution is. What your interviewer is looking for is evidence of your common sense, your ability to take decisions under pressure and your capacity to know your own limits.

Q. You are the manager of a large supermarket and you receive an anonymous telephone call saying that a number of the baby food products you carry have been tampered with by a protest group. How do you react?

A. I would suspect it was probably a hoax, but of course, I would take every precaution in case it were not. If I had an assistant, I would ask them to arrange to cordon off the baby food aisle and see what could be done to stop any items getting through the checkouts. I would also make a calm announcement over the PA. I would telephone the police and also local press and radio to begin a recall of any suspect items. If I had no assistant, my priority would be to stop anyone buying any of the products in question and then contact the police.

Q. You work for a company which has been involved in secret merger talks with another company — you are aware of this because it is your job to know, but you don't have any authority in these talks, or this deal. You are the last person in the office and you get a call from a member of the financial press saying that they have heard that this merger is taking place. What would you do?

A. I would say that they would have to speak to one of the directors of the company and that unfortunately none of them are available at the moment. I would check the diaries and give them the earliest possible time when they could call back again. If they pressed me, I would simply repeat my previous answer very calmly and very politely.

Q. You run the research and development section for your company and you have one designer in your section who is brilliant at his job, but very difficult to work with, unpredictable, bad tempered and unable to conform to the company rules on many occasions and yet there is no doubt he helps you make a lot of money because on a good day his ideas are brilliant. How do you deal with this?

A. I would have to look at whether we were losing other good staff because of him, how likely he would be to join one of our major competitors if we got rid of him, but most importantly whether there were things we could do to get him to work more effectively as a member of the whole team. I would start by talking to him and possibly involving the human resource department in this discussion and together we would all agree clear targets for improvements with a specific review period. I might also offer training and support if this seemed appropriate.

Tip

Get a friend to confront you with scenarios that they dream up (friends are capable of being far more sadistic than many real live interviewers). This will give you practice in marshalling your thoughts quickly.

Interviewers should not ask you questions about sex, religion and politics — indeed many of these questions are illegal and you will find some advice on this in the following chapter. They can, however, ask you questions about current affairs and general knowledge. Unless you are facing a particularly devious interviewer, these questions are not designed to reveal your political leanings, they are designed to test your ability to express your opinion, formulate an argument, defend a point of view. They won't usually pick really contentious issues. Expect questions such as the following.

Q. How would you improve the public transport system in this town/city?

Q. What steps would you take to integrate the student population more effectively into the local community?

Q. If you were suddenly given a million pounds to spend on improving this town, how would you spend it?

Q. How would you encourage more young people to continue with their education?

Q. Which story grabbed your attention in the news today?

Tip

You will need to be well prepared for these questions if you are going for a job in current affairs media, policy development, etc. You may also find you face this type of question related specifically to your own profession e.g., education, health, the environment the legal system, etc., so consider carefully the major issues and talking points within your profession at this moment.

That was horrible

There are some interviews where it is not so much the questions that hit a raw nerve with you, but problems about the interview itself. Silences, questions you just can't answer or unusually aggressive interviewers.

Silence may be golden, it may be a beautiful thing on a deserted beach under a starry sky but it loses its poetry and magic when it causes an embarrassing void in the flow of an interview conversation. To make matters worse, not all interview silence is the same kind of silence. There is the silence that means you have not got a clue what to say, the silence that means you know what the interviewer is getting at, but it is an awkward question and you need time to think about it or, the silence where you believe you have given a thorough, cogent and complete answer and yet your interviewer lets you down — he or she does not retort with the next question. In all three instances, resist the temptation to tell a joke, sing a song or rush out of the room in tears; there are more effective ways even than these to deal with the situation.

If you really don't know the answer to a question, then you should say so. This problem is most likely to occur if you are being asked technical/professional questions that you do not know the answers to at this stage, or if you are being asked to provide factual information of some kind.

A.   I am sorry, but that isn't an area I am familiar with at present, so I can't really give you any details on that.

A.   I am not familiar with that particular data management system, though I would imagine it is quite similar to others that I have used and I am usually quick to get to grips with new systems.

A.   I am sorry, but I haven't come across that particular term before, would you mind clarifying it for me?

A. I am afraid that is an area we did not cover on the course, but it is something I am very keen to learn more about.

A. I'm afraid that isn't a situation I have ever had to deal with, but I believe I would deal with it in the following way.

(Then go on to give specific details).

A. That is a new area for me, so I am afraid I can't really answer that. but I enjoy acquiring new knowledge and I do learn quickly.

A. That is not an area with which I am very familiar at the moment, but I see from your recruitment brochure that you offer a thorough induction programme and several training opportunities, so I would like to take advantage of one of these if I were to be offered a position with you.

A. I am not familiar with that legislation, but it is something I would make sure I brought myself up to speed on very quickly if you were to offer me this job.

A. I have never used that software before, but I would be happy to do any necessary training either through your training department or on an external course if that was more appropriate.

> **Tip**
>
> Replies like those above suggest a fair degree of personal confidence showing that you don't get flustered if there is something you don't know, so, not only do you get yourself out of a tight spot. You demonstrate your good qualities in action — self assurance, assertiveness, communication, honesty, eagerness to learn but be careful, you may become so carried away with this list that you make it a positive art form to stop knowing the answers to questions.

It is entirely acceptable to ask for clarification if you don't understand a question, though do this in a way that does not make your interviewer look silly. "I've no idea what you're on about" is not a response that will endear you to your interviewer.

A. I am sorry, I am not quite sure what you are asking. Could you ask me that question again please?

A. I am not sure where I should start with that, please could you give me a little bit more of an explanation?

Asking for a few moments to think about your answer can immediately remove the anxiety factor from a silence.

A. That's an interesting question, may I have a moment or two to collect my thoughts?

A. There is quite a lot I could say about that, can you bear with me while I think about that for a minute?

These responses are fine. Take it that you have overdone it if the interviewer goes away, makes a cup of coffee and deals with one or two vital telephone calls in the time you have taken to get your thoughts into some sort of order.

If you are faced with a situation where you think you have given a complete answer, but a silence ensues because you are not asked a further question, then you can always say

A. Is there anything you would like me to add?

A. Should I go on to tell you a little about how my previous job gave me some useful experience of dealing with these types of problems?

Encountering an aggressive interviewer is an unpleasant experience for a candidate to face. To some extent, this style of interview is currently out of fashion, but it could return at any moment, so it is wise to be prepared. Leaving aside the possibility that your interviewer simply has a personality problem, you have to ask yourself what is the rationale behind their decision to interview you in this way. It may be to determine how you react in a hostile situation and to discover aspects of your personality through other means than asking you to describe them. Keeping calm and avoiding hitting your adversary is a fundamental starting point. It is, however, important that you don't crumble under the pressure and that you do continue expressing your well-prepared answers clearly and assertively.

Tip

Aggressive sounding questions often begin with the word "Why". "Why did you take this decision?" "Why did this problem arise?" Just keep smiling as you answer the questions being fired at you and try not to take the whole thing too personally.

Remember the questions are not any more difficult, even if they are being asked in a rather unpleasant manner. It may be that the position you have applied for will mean that you are placed with some fairly aggressive colleagues or clients and if your interviewer is aware of this, they want to ascertain that you will be able to cope.

Once in a while, you are nice, your interviewer is pleasant, but circumstances are difficult. Your interview is constantly interrupted by telephone calls or by people bursting into the room. Your interviewer probably feels even more flustered than you by this, (unless it is some bizarre psychological test), but this is unlikely. Bad planning and time pressure or staff shortages are more likely explanations. Take a note of where the conversation broke off, so that you can get it back on track quickly if your interviewer is struggling with "and where were we?" One candidate being interviewed for a job at a company based in a coastal town had their interview interrupted because their interviewer was a member of the local lifeboat crew and he was summoned to a rescue — so some interruptions have to be forgiven.

Final tips for dealing with interview horrors

1. Prepare ahead for any areas where you know you may be vulnerable.

2. Ensure that those people whose names you are giving as referees know this beforehand and have given their permission for you to do so. This is not only courteous, but it means if there are any areas of concern, they may be prepared to discuss them with you in advance.

3. Accept that some interviews will go badly and you can't always redeem the situation.

4. Be candid and truthful, but don't give people information they don't ask for; you don't have to drag all the skeletons out of your cupboard.

5. Remember that you would never have been called for an interview if there was not a real chance that you could be the successful candidate, so be positive.

Chapter nine

a
level
playing field

equal opportunities, positive
thinking and the selection
process

Everyone who is called for an interview must accept that he or she might not be the best candidate. Unless you are going for a promotion within a company where you know which colleagues are applying too, or you are amongst a group of undergraduates all chasing the same company, the other candidates are an unknown quantity. What you do want to be assured of, however, is that you are being given a fair chance, that you haven't just been called to interview to make up the numbers and that the selection process will not discriminate against you on such grounds as age, gender, ethnic background or disability.

Whatever preparation you have undergone you cannot, as the one being interviewed, compensate either for the illegal actions or the poor attitude of interview panels, What you can do is to prepare yourself to be as positive and constructive as possible and also to at least be aware, if you find yourself being asked to answer what you regard as inappropriate or unacceptable questions. It is not within the scope of this book to offer a comprehensive guide to the law, but there are separate pieces of legislation concerning discrimination on grounds of gender, race and disability. There is no legislation regarding age discrimination, but the current Government has developed a Code of Practice on this and age as a cause for discrimination is likely to come under increasing scrutiny.

Employers are, of course, quite reasonably entitled to reassure themselves that you are capable of doing the job. Aware and experienced interviewers will ask questions in an *appropriate* way.

Q. With this job there are sometimes occasions when you have to work until 7.30 p.m. at short notice, would you be able to do that?

A. I understood this from your job description and it would not be a problem at all.

Rather than:

Q. I see you have children, what arrangements would you make for their care if you were required to work late?

This second version makes you feel you have to outline your childcare arrangements and diverts from the main purpose of the interview — to sell yourself. Try using an answer similar to the one above.

A. I considered all these issues carefully before I applied for this job, so I would be quite prepared to undertake this late work when it was necessary.

(In other words, it's none of your business, so long as I can fulfil my work commitments, but I am too polite and sensible to say so.)

An example of effective and poor ways of questioning an interviewee for whom English is not their first language.

Q. Tell me about your writing skills.

Q. How good are your verbal communication skills?

Rather than:

Q. I see from your CV that you only arrived in the UK two years ago and that English is not your first language, so how would you cope?

A. I had studied English at school, so my written English was reasonable before I arrived here. I have much preferred learning by using it though and I feel happy to hold a conversation on any subject. Actually, in one of my temporary administrative jobs I was complimented on my good command of the English language. I would be happy to learn other European languages too, it is something I enjoy and something that comes very easily to me.

Tip

You may believe that you have been asked an inappropriate or even illegal question in an interview, but common sense and your choice as an individual must dictate your reaction. You may still want the job and like everything else you have found out about the organization, in which case you may decide it is not appropriate to do anything other than answer the offending question as diplomatically and positively as you can. It is never easy to decide whether to be a trail blazer for the personal rights of yourself and other individuals or whether to follow the more pragmatic route.

Here are some examples of different ways of dealing with nasty questions.

Q. You don't mention your age on your CV — how old are you?

A. I am in my early 40s and I have had more than 20 years' work experience, the last five years in a human resource department and I believe all the experience I have had is very useful for this post. I have had so many opportunities to develop my interpersonal skills, working with other colleagues, different work teams and members of the public.

Q. You are older than most of the staff we employ here, how do you think you would fit in?

A. I think fitting in is all about personality and about a real interest in the job and has very little to do with age. I noticed that most of the staff in this agency, probably in most advertising agencies, are younger than me. I am comfortable working with any age group. I was the oldest student on my course, but I fitted in socially as well as academically — I have some creative ideas and after all, I have been a consumer for longer than most of your staff and know what makes me buy something.

Q. **The manager here is a lot younger than you, how do you feel about being managed by a younger person?**

A. I am far more interested in their qualities as a manager than in their age. I have had managers of various ages in the past and I have never found it to be an issue. I think it can be highly beneficial to have a mix of ages and types of experience — it provides a good opportunity for learning.

Q. **We hadn't realized you were so young when we called you for this interview, do you think you would be able to do the job?**

A. Of course, the job really appeals to me. I love sport and the idea of working at a leisure centre. I have had a lot of unpaid but really good experience, helping out with my family's retail business. I have often looked after the place on my own and I am very used to dealing with people.

Tip

There are some questions you should *never* feel obliged to answer, even if you do want to keep in your interviewer's good books. Questions such as "Have you ever been in love?" "Do you have a boyfriend/girlfriend?" "What is your sexual orientation?" "Do you practise any religion?" "Are you a member of a political party?" You would hope that interviewers would know better — but that is not always the case.

Q. **Are you married?**

(A question that really should not be asked.)

A. **1.** I am, but my working life and my home life are two separate things. I enjoy my current job very much, especially since I have taken on more management responsibility.

A.   **2.** No I am not, but married or not, my main current interest is in developing my career as an architect. I have followed your recent projects with a great interest and as you can see from my portfolio, my designs and aspirations seem to fit very well with what you are looking for.

A.   **3.** I don't really see the relevance of that question to this interview.

(You run the risk of sounding hostile with this third response, but that may be exactly how you feel and it may be the only response with which you feel comfortable.)

 Do you have children?

(This is another naughty one)

A.   **1.** No, I do not.

A.   **2.** Yes I do, two who are both at school. Having this dual role has made me a very effective time manager and it goes without saying that I am quite able to keep my domestic life and my working life well separated.

A.   **3.** I am not sure of the relevance of that question to my application for this position — I don't really feel comfortable answering such personal questions.

 From your CV, I see that you only arrived in this country three years ago — how are you fitting into the job market here?

A.   I am doing very similar work to that which I did before I came here — working on major construction projects and I have been qualified as a quantity surveyor for five years now. I am enjoying work here and if you were to offer me a job here I could be a great asset on some of your overseas projects later on.

Q. You have met staff in the office here, how well do you think you would fit in with us?

A. The staff I met seemed very friendly and very committed to family and community law. I would imagine that many of your clients in this locality are from different ethnic groups, so I would probably do your image a lot of good.

> **Tip**
>
> Never, ever, ever hit your interviewer, however tempting this may be. There are no recorded incidents of this being a successful tactic — unless, of course, interviewers are too proud to let on that they have succumbed.

It is understandable that interviewers will want to know how you are placed if either your job or the organization is likely to relocate or if there is a lot of travel involved.

Q. We are exploring the option of relocating our headquarters to another city, would you be able to relocate if we did?

A. Yes I would. I am established here and I am buying a local property, but if the job was right for me I would definitely be prepared to consider relocating. What kind of assistance do you provide for your staff in terms of a relocation package?

Q. If we offered you this job in our IT support department it would be necessary for you to provide some weekend cover and also to be on call for emergencies on a rota basis — do you have any problems with that?

A. That would be fine. In my current job I provide some weekend cover and I would be quite happy to continue this, I had anticipated it anyway. It would be useful to know how far in advance you plan your rotas, but I can usually be pretty flexible.

Q. How geographically mobile can you be?

A. I realize that this post could involve transfers and I bore that in mind when I applied. I like this area, but for the right opportunity I would undoubtedly consider moving.

Q. There is a lot of travel involved with this job, you would be away from home a lot, do you have any problems with that?

A. None at all. I simply see it as part of the work. I know it is not always as glamorous as it sounds, but I am pretty adaptable, good at getting on with work when I am not at my desk. I had to do a fair bit of that in my previous job.

Q. How long do you intend working for us?

A. I see this move as real career progress and if all goes well I would like to work here for the foreseeable future. I know that staff turnover can present real difficulties in social services and I feel it is important to stay put, to get to know the area, the clients and the department and the way it works. Ultimately, I would like to take on more management responsibility here.

Applicants with disabilities face particular concerns about the selection process. The full powers of the Disability Discrimination Act 1995 are yet to be realized, but many of its requirements concerning employment are already being put into effect. Job applicants with any disability, either physical or mental, do fear discrimination and also face a range of dilemmas about how and when to reveal their disability. If you have a disability and it is being discussed at your interview, the following questions and answers may assist you.

Q. You mentioned on your CV that you have had a health problem. Could you tell me a little more about that?

A. Yes, during my final year at university I developed ME and that is undoubtedly the reason why I got a third class degree, rather than the upper second which had been predicted. All my course work up to that time had received very high marks.

I am pleased to say, that it has responded very well to treatment and I am now feeling a great deal better, much more energetic and ready to take on full-time employment.

Q. You say on your application form that you are registered disabled and that you have a visual impairment. What implications would this have for us if we offered you a job?

A. I am sure it wouldn't have any implications for you. I would require a computer with a reasonably large screen and some specialized software, but you may already know that there is external funding available for that, so it would not have any cost implications for you. As far as doing the job is concerned, I am working successfully in a similar environment, though the job you are offering looks even more closely related to my MSc than the work I am currently doing.

Q. You mention that you are dyslexic — are there any ways in which you think this affects your work?

A. Well I must admit that spell checkers and other IT facilities are a marvellous invention as far as I am concerned, but as I work as a graphic artist my design skills and imagination are the key thing. I think one of the reasons they are as good as they are is because I have always had to find other ways than straightforward words to put my ideas across.

Disheartening as it is to anticipate prejudice or cultural bias, you may be able to pre-empt problems before they arise by considering what some of the assumptions in the minds of your interviewers might be.

Fighting misconceptions

- Women of child bearing age may soon go off on maternity leave.
- Women (and single men) with children may take a lot of time off to cope with domestic emergencies.

- Women may suddenly relocate to follow their partner's career moves.

- People with disabilities may cost the company money in terms of adaptations, special equipment, etc.

- If someone has a disability, they might take a lot of time off sick.

- Applicants from other ethnic groups may have cultural values that differ from those in this organization.

- We don't have a very diverse mix of staff here at the moment, so applicants from other backgrounds might not feel comfortable here.

- Qualifications and experience gained in another country probably won't be as useful as qualifications and experience acquired in this country.

- Black people are very aggressive.

- Older people won't learn as quickly.

- Older people won't cope with having a younger manager.

- Young people are likely to be restless and want to move on soon.

Tip

You don't need to prepare defensive answers to any of the above that you feel might apply to you. A more effective strategy is to bear these possible assumptions in mind when you are considering your skills, strengths, relevant experience and personal attributes, so that the selling points you put across, leave no room for these unfounded doubts in the minds of your interviewers.

Larger firms, government departments, local government departments and non-government organizations are likely to have a stated equal opportunities policy. This is not always the case among smaller organizations. This is not to imply that all large employers are good on equal opportunities while small ones are bad. It is easy to have a policy, but ensuring its implementation is a different question. A firm may have no stated policy and yet its ethos, attitude and commitment to equal opportunities may be laudable and genuine.

The way in which you are likely to experience the difference between the two, if you are called for an interview, is that larger organizations are may able to use trained interviewing staff, to have a standard set of questions that they ask all interviewees and to be in a position where they may be asked to justify their selection. Each candidate may be scored against specific selection criteria so that the interview panel can demonstrate that they have chosen the most suitable candidate.

Tip

When applying for positions with these larger organizations, you will often find that commitment to equal opportunities is one of the criteria mentioned on the person spec and one about which you will be questioned at interview. For example:

Q. Explain what you understand by an equal opportunities policy.

A. My understanding is that every employee and everyone with whom we deal will be treated fairly, regardless or age, gender, sexual orientation, ethnic and cultural background, disability or social background.

Questions and answers like these can lead to you feeling you have simply gone through every category you should on a check list. A more meaningful approach which you could encounter would be:

Q. What steps would you take to help implement our equal opportunities policy if we offered you a job in this department?

A. First of all, I would look at all the information we supply for our clients to answer two questions. First, is it accessible to everyone and second, does it carry positive images to represent all the different client groups we have? If the answer to either of these questions was "no" I would look at ways of improving access, not just on disability issues on things like leaflets in different languages more information available on our website. Those are just some initial thoughts.

The power of positive thinking

To some extent, interviewers believe what you tell them. This does not mean you can just make up any old collection of spurious qualifications and imaginary periods of employment, but they won't normally argue that an experience is insignificant or irrelevant if you have described it as valuable. They won't challenge your assertion that you possess a certain quality, so long as you can offer evidence of an occasion when you used or developed it.

For this reason, the more positive you are about dealing with any doubts, stated overtly or hinted at covertly during your interview, the better the impression that you will make. Being mature equals wisdom, common sense and breadth of experience. Being from a different background denotes different ways of looking at things, new ideas, the overcoming of obstacles and the opportunity to bring valuable diversity to a workforce. Train all your thoughts and your preparation in this direction and the boost this will give to your self confidence is almost guaranteed to rub off on your interviewer.

Final tips on working towards fair play

1. What can you find out about your prospective employer's attitude to equal opportunities? Do they mention it in their advert, do they have a stated policy? What kind of images do you see on their website and in their other publicity?

2. Amass all your positive selling points exactly as you have done for any other aspect of the interview, but paying special attention to areas that you see as potentially sensitive.

3. Learn how to be assertive and ensure that you know how to distinguish this from being aggressive. Avoid being passive.

4. Be confident in articulating your selling points.

5. Be realistic, you may have given a weak interview — try to assess where the fault really lies.

6. If you feel that you really have been treated unfairly and on discriminatory grounds, then seek professional advice.

Chapter ten

turning the tables

tables

your questions answered — you in control

"Is there anything you would like to ask me?" This question frequently arises towards the end of an interview and it is another of those questions that candidates worry about. Supposing you haven't thought of anything, what if all the questions you have so carefully prepared have been answered by the extensive and relevant information you have been given during your interview or through informal conversations with other employees before your interview?

If you really feel that everything that you want to know has been covered fully elsewhere, then say so, as politely as possible. Versions of some of the following may ease your anxiety.

A.   Your graduate recruitment brochure is really informative and it answers all the questions I have about the company and about what I might expect my work to involve, how my work performance would be assessed and what I can expect for the future if I put in the effort and commitment.

A.   Thank you, but I have been able to find so much out from your website, it has been a really useful way to find answers to all my questions. It is a very well-designed site and so easy to navigate.

A. I was able to find out so much from your colleagues when we had our tour of the production line and offices this morning, that I don't think there is anything else I need to ask you at the moment thank you.

There are no prizes for asking really obscure and difficult questions, least of all, those questions which might make you look smarter than your interviewer — that doesn't go down well. If you have learned their annual turnover figures for the past decade or know the names of every member of staff in the post room, keep this to yourself and take note that with such a brilliantly trained memory, you may have a great future in pub quiz teams.

> **Tip**
>
> Remember this opportunity for you to ask your own questions is not only there to see what you have thought of, it is a real chance for you to seek clarification or further information on aspects of the work, the organization and your potential role within that organisation — it is a good opportunity — so take advantage of it.

Preparing before the interview can help you to come up with some sensible questions which indicate that you are both intelligent in your approach to the job and have throughout seriously about your possible future within that set up, your training needs your prospects and how the company might reward your efforts. The majority of the interview is dedicated to allowing the company to assess whether they think you have got what it takes — it is perfectly reasonable that you should want to know whether they have got what it takes to satisfy your choices, ambitions and goals.

Use the questions below to develop your own questions related to the specific job you are applying for.

Q. What are some of your current major projects?

Q. What projects/campaigns/developments do you have planned for the future that you are able to talk about?

Q. Which projects would the successful candidate be working on initially?

Q. To what extent am I likely to be working on my own?

Q. To what extent am I likely to be working as part of a team and are staff involved in more than one project team at the same time?

Q. To what extent would I have the opportunity to use and develop my language skills?

(Clearly you can substitute any relevant skill here, information technology, supervisory, research, etc. Whichever are pertinent for you and might logically be developed as part of your role within the organization.)

Q. What kind of training will I be given if I am offered this job?

(You should be able to make this mention of training more specific, e.g., management training, training on your computer system, customer care training, or whatever is relevant to the position concerned.)

Q. Do you encourage staff to take relevant professional qualifications?

Q. What support, if any, do you give to staff who take further professional qualifications?

Q. What is your policy on staff development?

Q. How much contact am I likely to have with other departments/external organizations/clients/customers?

Q. Are there particular management models which you favour?

Q. In which of your offices is the position based initially?

Q. How much autonomy can I expect to be given within my work?

Q. How much of a requirement is there to be geographically mobile? How soon would I be expected to relocate?

Q. Are there likely to be any opportunities for overseas travel/ travel within the UK?

Q. What approximate starting salary do you have in mind?

Q. Are salary reviews performance related?

Q. When might I expect my first salary review?

Q. What salary progression might I reasonably expect over the first three years?

> **Tip**
>
> It is debatable as to when is the most appropriate moment to raise questions about your salary, you can always save these for a telephone conversation or a further meeting once you have been offered the job. If, however, a starting salary has been discussed, it is entirely reasonable that you should want to find out how much better it is likely to get and how soon.

Q. Do you have a formal appraisal system?

Q. If everything goes well, where might I expect to be in two/three/five years' time?

Q. How soon could I reasonably anticipate a promotion?

Q. What are some typical career paths of graduates you have taken on in the last two years?

You may have questions concerning such matters as housing or living costs in the areas, availability of suitable housing, local schools, etc., if you would have to relocate in order to take up the job. It is not unreasonable to ask about these things, but don't take up too much time on these issues — this is very much the kind of information you can glean from other members of staff either before or after your interview in a more informal setting.

> **Tip**
>
> Don't allow yourself to become so desperate to ask a question that you resort to "What sort of quality cappuccino can I expect from your vending machines?" "Does someone have to die before I get a space in the company car park?" Your questions should reflect a genuine interest in the company and/or a sense that if you are successful you intend to stay around for some time, that you are thinking in the longer term, not only about what your immediate salary, training and situation will be on taking up your post.

Nice and easy

Easy yes, but not necessarily nice. One situation that can come as a bit of a surprise in an interview, is the interview where you feel you really haven't been asked much at all and haven't been given the inquisitorial grilling you anticipated and prepared for. After the initial relief a few minutes into the interview, you should start considering what is going on and whether there is anything you can or should do about it. There are several possible explanations for the interview taking this form.

The first and most pessimistic prognosis is that the interviewer has already switched off and so won't invest any energy in finding out more. Perhaps they have already seen a candidate who has impressed them so much that all your efforts are in vain or that rapport, that sparkle, simply isn't there. You can usually tell if this is the case as the interview is short and you are asked very few follow-up questions which encourage you to expand on your replies. More than this, your own gut feelings warn you that this is a lost cause.

The second and most optimistic possibility is that you have hit it off really well with the interviewer, you are that candidate who is going to render your competitors' efforts useless. Your future employer is already convinced that you are the ideal recruit and aside from making sure there are no dreadful skeletons in your cupboard, they see no need to pursue the matter any further.

Delightful as this scenario is, do not allow yourself to bask in a smug state of certainty, carry on putting a real effort into your performance — another sparkling candidate could be about to enter the room just as you leave it.

Unrelated to the two reasons above is the likelihood that the interviewer simply is not very skilled in questioning, they may have had limited experience of conducting selection interviews and may be unaware of how to get the right information. You are less likely to encounter this situation if you are being interviewed by a large company or organization where there is a human resource department and where managers are trained and experienced in all aspects of the recruitment process. You might encounter inexperienced interviewers with a small company, or if you are sent for a technical interview if you have been successful at your initial interview. You may be someone's first ever candidate or they may be jaded by years and years of recruitment interviewing.

The third option is the one where there is the greatest opportunity for you to take the initiative — the first is probably a lost cause and with the second you have very little to worry about. The reason that you need to take the initiative is that it is all very well feeling that you have come out of an interview having learned everything about the history of the company and the personal circumstances of your questioner, but if they have treated other candidates in exactly the same way then how do they come to make their selection when they have interviewed every candidate?

Here are some possible questions or comments that you could make which begin to distinguish you from the crowd. You do need to ensure that you don't offend the interviewer, by cutting them off in mid flow, so wait for a pause, but be prepared to jump in quickly before they start up all over again.

Q. **It sounds as if the company has had a really interesting history. Where do you see it going in the next year or two?**

Always appear interested in what your interviewer is saying, even if they are rambling on and on and you are feeling frustrated at not being able to sell yourself, lean forward and look enthusiastic, this also gives them a clue that you want to say something.

Q. It sounds as if you really enjoy working here, who would I be working with if you took me on?

Q. Yes, your latest product range is impressive, the things I particularly like about it are . . .

Q. It is interesting that you say you much prefer working for a smaller set up like this. I would really like to make the move to a smaller company where whatever my specific responsibilities, I could feel far more involved and have a much greater understanding of everything we do and that is very much how you describe your role here.

Q. What you say about that recent project sounds really interesting. I really enjoyed the marketing project I did in the final year of my course because it took me out of university and gave me opportunities to meet several people from the industry — it gave me a real basis for comparison when I started making my job applications and although I didn't visit your company as part of my project I really like what I have found out about you and particularly all the useful information you have given me this morning.

You can also grab the opportunity when asked "is there anything else you would like to ask me?" Turn the situation around with a reply such as:

A. Well, I don't actually have any questions, as you have given me a great deal of useful information, but there are one or two points I would like to make, if I may, that highlight some aspects of my current work which are extremely relevant to the post I am applying for.

A. Not exactly questions, but I would like to tell you a little bit about a project I undertook while I was a student which looked at how to develop better customer after care for services like the one you provide.

Nightmare to avoid

One candidate took his quest for control to such an extent that he took to whispering the word "me" whenever the interviewer used phrases like "the person we appoint" or "the successful candidate". His attempt to tap into the deeper levels of his interviewer's consciousness did no good whatsoever, since she assumed he was at best a little odd and at worst ... well, sinister would be an understatement.

Tip

In an ideal interview, you, as candidate should be speaking for approximately 80 per cent of the time. Again, it is one of those situations where you have, to a great extent, to be guided by your intuition — you will sense when it is acceptable to take control of a conversation and begin adding some points of your own, if the interviewer has failed to give you a chance to shine. Remember they may just be extremely tired — if they have been interviewing several candidates on the same day they will have had to concentrate, to think, to communicate and to be prepared to take important decisions.

Poacher turned game keeper

There is one kind of interview where you are very much in control — information gathering interviews, where you set up the interview in order to find out more about a particular organization or, more often, a particular type of work — quantity surveyor, retail buyer, occupational therapist or curator of meteorites (yes, there is such a job).

These information gathering interviews are especially useful if you are at the point of making a career decision, be that on leaving school, university or college or a change of direction somewhere along your career path.

You arrange the interview yourself, requesting someone to spend a little of their time talking to you about their work and what it involves. You can do this by writing or telephoning likely people or organizations or, if you are lucky, you may have friends or contacts within your selected profession who can help out with this.

Tip

Don't be afraid to try this, it is amazing how many people, even busy people, are happy to talk about their work, they often find it enjoyable to have a fresh and eager audience to hear about their woes, their joys, the idiosyncrasies of their boss, etc and you have nothing to lose by trying something like this. At worst, you won't find anyone willing to talk to you and that may, in itself, tell you something about the industry or business you think you are about to enter.

Nightmare to avoid

An applicant considering training in midwifery telephoned what she believed was her local hospital midwifery department to ask whether she could come in and talk about the work and perhaps help out a little bit in the department. She had actually got through to her local university library, where the chief librarian readily acceded to her request. It was only when she said she hoped she could witness a few births, perhaps including at least one caesarean, that the penny dropped. If you are arranging to talk to someone about their work and your career, make sure you really do know who you are talking to.

If you do arrange any such interviews yourself you will find that you are asking some similar questions to those outlined in Chapter 3 on employment history, though you are likely to find that your information gathering discussion takes on a much more informal tone than a selection interview. Nevertheless, it helps to have some prepared questions, it gives the person you are talking to the sense that you value their time and it helps you ensure that you really do get the sort of information that is going to be useful to you.

You may find some of the following prompts useful.

Q. How long have you worked here?

Q. What does your actual day-to-day work involve?

Q. Could you describe a typical day or a typical week for me, if there is such a thing in this job?

Q. What do you most enjoy about working here?

Q. What are the things that are most difficult to deal with in your job?

Q. How typical do you think this firm/school/Civil Service department/ agency is? Have you worked for any others?

Q. How approachable is the management here?

Q. Would you recommend someone to enter this profession?

Q. What do you think it takes to be really successful in this job?

Q. What are the opportunities like for career progression either here or by moving to similar organizations?

Q. What is the working atmosphere like here? Do you tend to socialize with colleagues outside working hours?

Q. Is there much opportunity to get further training? What sort of attitude is there to staff development?

Q. What are the major issues that you feel this profession/this company/this business has to face over the next few years?

Q. What significant changes have you seen since you started work in this industry/profession?

As well as becoming more well informed by conducting such information gathering interviews, there is also a possibility that you can turn the situation to your advantage by making useful contacts who, even if they are not in a position to offer you employment then and there, are impressed enough to bear you in mind for the future or can put you in touch with contacts of their own, who may be able to offer you something. You can begin to build up a network, within your chosen career which will lead to future selection interviews, rather than information interviews.

Tip

Be pleasant, persistent and enthusiastic in your quest for this information, it really is worth the time and trouble.

Final tips to help you take control

1. Prepare your questions in advance, either for an information interview or a selection interview.

2. Remind yourself of your main selling points, so that if nobody asks you about them you are prepared to grab opportunities to mention them.

3. Remember that these situations provide a wonderful chance for you to demonstrate your very good interpersonal skills in action.

Chapter eleven

summing
up

learning from every interview,
planning for your next encounter
and dealing with unusual
interviews

Your interview is behind you and unlike exams you don't meet the rest of the candidates in the corridor, saying they have revised the wrong bit or that they can't believe how easy it was. You are even spared the one person who declares that they have failed and the whole thing was a complete disaster, while you and everyone else in the class knows that they will get the top mark for the year.

You have the luxury of dealing with your reactions in private, but on most occasions, you also have the anxiety of a wait of anything between a few hours and a few days. This is dependent on if and when they are seeing other candidates and also on whether other staff are involved in the decision, maybe human resources finance or other line managers have a say.

Whatever the situation, don't let your performance in the closing minutes of the interview disintegrate through a sense of relief, optimism gloom or exhaustion, keep sparkling until the last handshake and the parting smile is over and the interview room door is closed firmly behind you.

Thoughtful interviewers will remember to tell you what the time frame for their decision is likely to be and when and how successful candidates are to be informed, and whether or not they contact unsuccessful candidates too. If they don't impart this information, summon up the courage to ask this at the end of your interview.

Q. When will you be able to let me know the result of this interview please?

Q. Do you usually telephone or write to the successful candidate?

Q. Do you normally contact the candidates who have not been successful?

Q. You do have my telephone number, mobile, etc., if you need to get in touch with me?

Nightmare to avoid

One candidate was so desperate to know the result of his interview that he told the panel he was going on holiday for three weeks that evening, so could they possibly let him know now. He wasn't and they did. He hadn't got the job.

If you know that other candidates are being seen over the coming few days you could write a letter after your interview, thanking your interviewer for their time, stating what interested you and confirmed your enthusiasm for the job and reminding them of some of your key selling points. A letter such as this is unlikely to clinch a decision one way or the other, but it can do no harm and it may just put you back in their minds when they come to sum up all the candidates and review their notes.

Always thank your interviewer(s) before you leave, maintain your poise and breezy confidence and tell them you have found the interview interesting/very useful/enjoyable/it has confirmed and increased your enthusiasm for the post, the work, the organization — whatever words you can find that sound neither too false or too pleading, but which leave a positive impression as you depart from the room.

There are two possible results to any job interview, either you get the job or you do not. There are others, you are the second choice and their first choice turns them down, they can't offer you anything now, but they will in the future if they can, etc., but these constitute a minority of cases.

> **Tip**
>
> If you are offered the job on the spot it is best to accept it enthusiastically (unless of course you know you are definitely not interested). You may want to spend the evening thinking about it, talking it through with family members or friends, but if you seem indecisive at the interview you may miss the boat. One word of caution — don't give your acceptance in writing unless you really are sure you want the job.

Not being offered a job, particularly if it was one that you really wanted very much is a painful experience and all the following advice and suggestions on assessing your performance and planning for the future does recognize that it can be a real disappointment.

> **Tip**
>
> Do not assume that just because you did not get the job you are a total disaster and a complete failure. Few of us have only one friend, deem only one holiday destination as suitable or only like one dish on a menu, so why should only one candidate be suitable for a job?

Among the many potential reasons for not being offered a job after an interview are:

1. You were fine, but another candidate was better.
2. Perhaps you would have been the best person for the job, but interviews are always a slightly hazy selection tool and they don't always choose the most suitable person.
3. You and the interviewer simply didn't have that certain rapport.
4. It was a very close run thing between you and another candidate and in the end the selection boiled down to luck as much as to judgement.

5. Other candidates were better prepared overall, for the interview and thus more able to convey their suitability to the interviewer.

6. The selector(s) decided that on this occasion, none of the applicants were suitable.

7. There were questions in the interview which you found difficult to answer.

8. Your overall interview performance was not that brilliant — you just didn't have that sparkle on the day.

Many of the above reasons are beyond your control, but you are well placed to tackle the final two, examining how well prepared you were overall and asking yourself whether there were specific questions that you could have answered more effectively and with more panache if you had been better armed to face them.

It is hard when you first leave the interview, because though it is fresh in your mind, you are tired and whatever gut feelings you have about the result, you don't actually know whether or not you have been successful. Nevertheless, you must use this time when the experience is still in your recent memory to take a little time to sit down, reflect coolly on your performance, and make sure that if necessary, you can do even better next time.

Tip

It would be helpful if all interviewers were willing to give feedback on candidates' interview performance and some are, but it is a delicate issue for a candidate. If you ask at the end of your interview whether the person or panel is prepared to give feedback on your performance it can feel like a wearisome prospect for the interviewer and it can convey a sense that you have already decided you have not been successful and leave a negative impression, so approach this one with caution. Kind and not-too-busy interviewers sometimes contact a candidate who really was a close second to let them know how well they did, but merely mentioning this may cause mass paranoia among applicants who have recently attended interviews and heard nothing.

After you have left the interview and at least allowed yourself a cup of tea or coffee, large bar of chocolate or whatever is your particular indulgence, review your interview critically.

What were the names and positions within the organization of the person or people who interviewed you? You may be speaking to them again.

What was the agreed arrangement for informing candidates of the outcome?

Is there likely to be a follow-up interview, personality or aptitude test or any other additional form of selection to build on this initial interview?

Were there questions for which you were not well prepared and how would you prepare for these in the future?

Were there questions which you answered well, what made these successful in your eyes and how can you translate this success to your weaker topics?

How great a part did your nerves play in your overall performance?

Did you find out whether other opportunities are likely to arise with the organization, even if you were not successful on this occasion?

Were you able to get satisfactory answers to your own questions?

What lasting impression do you think you made during your interview? Were you quiet and shy, or did you come over as friendly and confident?

What was the most difficult question you had to answer?

Did you take the opportunity to ensure that you got your key selling points across?

Would you really have liked the job?

Have you gained any new insight into the organization, its work, your chosen career?

Have you gained any new personal insight?

The point of going through these questions is not to encourage you into masochistic waves of self doubt and gloom, nor indeed to confirm that all interviewers are mean and narrow minded and just haven't seen you for the wonderful and capable person you really are. It is to ensure that you give an even better performance next time.

In a perfect world, we would be able to test out our interview techniques on employers who weren't really our first choice, so that these served as dress rehearsals for the ones we really care about. Providence is not always so generous, so you must treat every interview as if it really matters — after all, you can always turn the job down if the employer doesn't come up to scratch.

Having reviewed your performance using the questions above, make notes on these and draw up an action plan to enhance your future interview success.

What research should I do next time and what resources can I use?

For which questions do I need to work out better answers?

Are there any aspects of my personal performance I need to improve on, e.g., being more assertive, trying to do more to combat my nerves?

Interviews with a difference

While the interviewing organization's premises is the standard venue for selection interviews, there is always the possibility the you will be invited to an interview in a more informal setting such as a hotel or a restaurant and some employers use no premises at all — they interview you on the telephone.

Telephone interviews are used either by large organizations that are recruiting several staff at the same time and can use the fairly brief telephone interview as a first stage of selection (most commonly after receipt of a CV or application form), or by companies recruiting staff whose work will necessitate them having a good telephone manner, telesales or call centre work, for example.

If you know you are facing a telephone interview, you should prepare to sell yourself in exactly the same way as you do for a face to face meeting, but you must also develop the additional skill of sounding convincing without relying on any of the non verbal clues and cues you would normally give — your friendly smile, your firm handshake, the confident way in which you take your seat, or the way that you maintain good eye contact with your interviewer. You need to concentrate on putting feeling and enthusiasm into your tone of voice. Obviously you should use this in ordinary interviews too, but it is even more crucial when your voice is all the interviewer has to go on, apart from what is written on your CV.

Tip

Get a friend to help you with this exercise. Either telephone them, or if you are in the same room, sit back to back, so that they have no visual clues. Pick some entirely neutral words, for example numbers between 1 and 20. Think of an emotion and say one of these neutral words trying to convey that feeling, pleasure, irritation, enthusiasm, anger, etc. and see if the friend can label the emotions correctly. When talking to employers stick to the pleasure and enthusiasm the anger and irritation are only to help you develop your technique.

You may feel foolish, but you could also try calling your own answerphone and leaving a message just to see exactly how you sound. You should rehearse exactly what you are going to say at the start of the call, especially if you have been asked to telephone the employer — the impression you give as you introduce yourself is very important.

If you are initiating what could turn out to be a telephone interview, for example, telephoning an employer to see if they have vacancies or just to ask who you should address your enquiries to, you should still have a ready prepared 'script', you may have called at an opportune moment when they are thinking of expanding or when a member of staff has just handed in their notice and your tentative enquiry could turn instantly into a selection interview.

Tip

Your script should be rather like the essential points on your CV, though concentrating most particularly on what attracts you to the job/company/type of work, plus your relevant experience and qualities and your suitability and motivation. The hard part is fitting that into no more than thirty seconds, but it is worth doing and worth practising. Friends, who come in handy for so many aspects of interview preparation, can help out yet again.

Nightmare to avoid

Several telephone interviewees have been so determined to deliver their scripts that they have forgotten to check who they are speaking to on the other end of the telephone. Your takeaway won't arrive any faster because the local restaurant now knows that you are a fully qualified and highly motivated environmental technologist and the company's cleaning contractor may think you sound lovely, but is unlikely to have the power to offer you employment.

Telephone interviews are quite difficult, but look on the bright side, at least you don't have to spend time and money on your interview wardrobe on this occasion.

Food, drink and 'informality'

Most interviews take place in offices, alright they may occasionally resemble broom cupboards, but they are still official work premises. Some interviews do take place in cafés, restaurants and bars, and these place candidates under considerable strain. You still want to get your key selling points across and convince your interviewer that you are the right person for this job, while deciding how expensive a dish you dare order from the menu, what attitude to take to the consumption of alcohol and whether to tell your interviewer that they have parsley stuck between their teeth. On top of all this you don't want everyone else to hear you explaining why you are the best investment manager, pensions analyst/financial futures dealer that ever walked the planet. These examples have been used because this type of recruitment is not common for teachers, nurses or prison officers. Keep your fingers crossed that none of the general public on this occasion includes any friends or colleagues of yours.

The only advice that can really help here is sticking rigorously to all the common rules of courtesy that would apply when you are out eating or drinking. Don't order expensive or messy food and avoid ordering anything if you are not sure exactly what it is. Don't forget all your interview preparation — it is just as relevant here as anywhere else. Don't be lulled into a false sense of security by the surroundings your 'interviewer' even if he or she has called it an informal meeting or a friendly chat, will still be working hard to assess whether you are the right person, whether you will fit in.

Even rarer than the 'informal' interview is the highly disconcerting situation where, for example, two candidates are interviewed at the same time — yes, in the same room — and have to compete to make the best impression. There are instances of ad agencies or PR consultants using this technique from time to time, but it is so uncommon that you need not lie awake at night wondering if it will happen to you. If it does, exactly the same rules apply as for any other interview — it is just that assertiveness and self confidence will be two skills that are tested very directly.

Your future interviews

Interview technique is, without question, something which you can improve with practice and job interviews are something that we face throughout our working lives. Most interviews happen for the best reasons; you want a change, you want to move on, you want a new challenge you have completed your education or training. Even those interviews that you have been obliged to go for perhaps because of loss of a job or some other misfortune, are at least evidence that you are moving in the right direction — you are saying the right things on your written application.

Before you attend your next interview

- Ensure that you have acted on your action plan; that is why they are so named.

- Be honest with yourself about your potential and your suitability for this next position you have applied for.

- Ensure that you have carried out any reasonable research about the work, the organization and the specific post you have applied for.

- Practise your interview technique with a friend, especially those questions that caught you out in any previous interviews.

- It is difficult, but try to look forward to the interview and see it is something you will enjoy.

- Be philosophical. If you don't get this next one, perhaps you would not have liked the job anyway and there will always be other interviews.

Luck, providence, fate, whatever you wish to call it, always plays a certain role in the whole process of interviews and job seeking, so may it be on your side and give you that little bit extra in addition to all your own hard work and thorough preparation.

Index of questions

Questions about education and qualifications

Questions about work experience and employment history

Questions to find out what you know about the organizations you are applying to

Questions concerning weaknesses and perceived failures

Problem solving or scenario questions

Current affairs questions

Questions concerning equal opportunities (some illegal)

Questions for your own information gathering interviews